Power to the People!

RICHARD PANCHYK

Fighting for our Rights
as Citizens and Consumers

Power to the People!

SEVEN STORIES PRESS
New York · Oakland · London

A TRIANGLE SQUARE BOOK FOR YOUNG READERS
PUBLISHED BY SEVEN STORIES PRESS

SEVEN STORIES PRESS
140 Watts Street
New York, NY 10013
www.sevenstories.com

College professors and high school and middle school teachers may order
free examination copies of Seven Stories Press titles.
Visit https://www.sevenstories.com/pg/resources-academics or
email academics@sevenstories.com.

Library of Congress Cataloging-in-Publication Data
NAMES: Panchyk, Richard, author.
TITLE: Power to the people! : how tort law keeps us safe from
corporations, a young adult's guide / Richard Panchyk.
DESCRIPTION:New York, NY : Seven Stories Press, [2020] | Series: For young
people | Includes bibliographical references. | Audience: Ages 10-14
IDENTIFIERS: LCCN 2020050687 (print) | LCCN 2020050688 (ebook) |
ISBN 9781644210888 (trade paperback) | ISBN 9781644210895 (epub)
SUBJECTS: LCSH: Tort liability of corporations--United States--Juvenile
literature. | Torts--United States--Juvenile literature.
CLASSIFICATION: LCC KF1301.A2 P36 2020 (print) |
LCC KF1301.A2 (ebook) | DDC 346.7303--dc23
LC record available at https://lccn.loc.gov/2020050687
LC ebook record available at https://lccn.loc.gov/2020050688

Book design by Stewart Cauley and Abigail Miller

Printed in the USA.

9 8 7 6 5 4 3 2 1

Contents

Acknowledgments

I OFFER A VERY SPECIAL AND HEARTFELT thanks to Ralph Nader, who has been an inspiration, a mentor, a teacher, and a friend, for truly believing in me and in my work over the last fifteen years. His optimistic persistence and his deep commitment to tort law and empowering the average citizen made this book possible. Thanks to Rick Newman at the Museum of American Tort Law for his help and encouragement. Thanks to John Richard for providing some images for the book. And of course, thanks to Dan Simon at Seven Stories Press for believing in the importance of this project.

Preface

EVERYTHING GOOD IN THIS WORLD STARTS
with one person.

Every innovation, every movement for a
better country and a better planet, begins with
just one person.

Yes, it often does take many people to make
a change happen, but the seeds of change start
with you and me. The seeds of change start
with a single idea: a thought, a hope, a vow, a
dream. From there, a movement can grow and
one person's voice can become a chorus of tens,
hundreds, thousands—a chorus that will be
heard loud and clear by the powers that be.

In this book, you'll read about how one
person CAN make a difference in fighting
against injustice, starting with the story of a
man who inspired generations of Americans to

take action. You'll read about how corporations became powerful and took over the country, and how we can all fight to take our country back and protect our rights as citizens. You'll learn about tort law and how our Constitution guarantees us the right to challenge even the largest corporations when we have been wronged.

Hopefully, you'll be inspired to become an involved citizen and understand how you can be heard, whether in a court of law, at the ballot box, or within a group of like-minded people. We can make a difference, all of us. Embrace your hopes and never believe that you have no voice or power. You do. I do. We all do.

CHAPTER ONE

RALPH NADER AND THE FIGHT FOR CONSUMER PROTECTION

THE TALL, THIN MAN WALKED BRISKLY ALONG THE *sidewalk, well aware he was being watched. This had been going on for some time now, and he knew exactly who was following him. He'd recently made an enemy, and it wasn't just one person. No, his enemy was an entire company—one of the largest and most powerful companies in America. As he turned to go into his building, the man knew his stalker was taking photos of him from across the street. Let him snap away, the man told himself. That won't frighten me from my mission. I may be just one person, but no company is going to intimidate me, no matter how big they are. I am going to fight this—and win!*

I

From the way it's shown in old movies and television shows, you'd think that the 1950s was a carefree time in America.

Maybe it was in some ways. There were exciting, stylish cars, drive-in movies, roadside diners, and a new craze called "rock and roll" music. There was a lot that made the decade seem "cool." But life was not all fun and games. There was also a lot of danger in everyday life back then. For one thing, almost half of the adult population smoked cigarettes in the 1950s. And they smoked everywhere—in offices, homes, restaurants, and even on airplanes. Even if you yourself didn't smoke, you inhaled plenty of smoke anyway. The cars sure looked nice, but they were unsafe in many ways and caused many thousands of preventable deaths every year. Even the toys that 1950s kids played with were hazardous.

Few people took note of any of these hazards of everyday living with a determination to do something about them.

Until, that is, a New England native named Ralph Nader came onto the scene. It was during the late 1950s that Nader, a young lawyer from a small town called Winsted in northern

Connecticut, began to take a careful look at the dangers all around him.

Born to Lebanese immigrant parents, Nader had taken an early interest in the law and government while still in elementary school. His parents were eager to feed his curiosity and brought him to observe local county courtroom trials, and town meetings in Winchester. "They let us observe and afterward ask questions or make comments as part of dinner table discussions," said Nader, of how he and his siblings were treated. Learning how to listen was a key part of Nader's childhood. By listening, he learned a great deal—listening to his parents' stories about their past, listening to their guests, listening to the news on the radio, listening to his teachers.

He was also very much in touch with nature as a kid. He enjoyed the fruit trees in his New England yard, the vegetable garden where his family grew tomatoes, lettuce, beans, cucumbers, radishes, and squash, and the dense woods he crossed to get to school. This appreciation for nature helped mold his later desire to protect the environment from pollution and destruction. He also learned to love history and to appreciate the local landmarks in his hometown. His mother encouraged him to be an independent thinker; a leader had to think independently to be innovative. "Turn your back on the pack," she would tell him.

Another thing driven into his head at a young age was to appreciate and favor family-run businesses over chain stores. For example, his father stayed away from the local A&P supermarket, telling him it was better to shop at small businesses than places run by large corporations—a preference that stuck with the boy as he grew up.

Nader knew, even as a kid, that he wanted to be an attorney. His political heroes included Eugene Debs (a labor organizer and five-time presidential candidate between 1900 and 1920), Senator Robert Lafollette (reformer, leader of the Progressive movement, and 1924 presidential candidate), Thomas Paine (author of an influential Revolutionary War era pamphlet called *Common Sense*), Norman Thomas (a pacifist minister who ran for president six times starting in 1928), Thomas Jefferson, and Benjamin Franklin.

As a teenager, Nader was an avid reader and devoured book after book. Many of the books he read were about social activists of the early twentieth century, people who exposed dangerous conditions in this country and tried to change them for the better. These books were as exciting and interesting to the young man as a murder mystery novel would be to others. There was something very inspiring in the stories of average people who took a stand against injustice and actually made a difference, against the odds. One of these "muckrakers," as they were called, was the novelist and journalist Upton Sinclair, who wrote a novel called *The Jungle* that exposed the terrible conditions in meatpacking plants at the turn of the twentieth century.

By the time Nader left his hometown to go off to college, he had a fire in his belly, a strong desire to make a difference in the world. He graduated from Princeton University in 1955 and went on to study at Harvard University, where he got his law degree in 1958. Understanding the law and practicing law helped him learn how to have an effect on the world around him.

While he was a student at Princeton, Nader would often hitchhike, and it was on these rides with truck drivers that he happened to be first on the scene of occasional car accidents. In those terrible and tragic scenes, he began to see the various things that needed to be changed about cars, including the way cars crumpled and the way occupants were hurled through the windshield or impaled by the steering column. Cars of the era seemed to offer little protection to their occupants when it mattered most! They were fun to drive and pretty to look at—but in an accident, they were deadly. Not only that, these cars were actually prone to accidents such as rolling over. Why did it have to be that way? There was no good reason for cars to be that unsafe.

To make matters worse, some of his friends had been injured in terrible car accidents like the kind he'd seen. Nader began to study cars and automobile safety, and his research uncovered many issues in automobile design that caused serious injury or death. He wrote his third-year paper at Harvard on unsafe cars and liability, called "Unsafe Auto Design and the Law." It was quite a new topic as there was not much previously written about automobile safety.

After receiving his law degree, Nader got a job as an attorney handling ordinary legal issues and paperwork, but consumer safety was still on his mind. All the while, he remained focused on his automotive safety research. In 1959, Nader wrote an article titled "The Safe Car You Can't Buy," which was published in the *Nation*. In the article he wrote: "It is clear Detroit today is designing automobiles for style, cost, performance and calculated obsolescence, but not—despite the 5,000,000 reported accidents, nearly 40,000 fatalities, 110,000 permanent disabilities and 1,500,000 injuries yearly—for safety."

His initial research paper and article led to several more years of intensive research, and finally, to the publication of his groundbreaking first book, *Unsafe at Any Speed: The Designed-In Dangers of the American Automobile*. The book revealed the many ways auto makers had chosen style or horsepower over safety, resulting in thousands of unnecessary deaths and injuries every year and numerous lawsuits filed against General Motors (GM) relating to Corvair injuries. The effect was sudden and rapid— Nader's book was published November 30, 1965 (a few weeks before the book was published, the *Nation* adapted a chapter of his book as an article titled "Profits versus Engineering—The Corvair

Story"), and less than a month later, GM was the defendant in numerous lawsuits.

Nader, who had been an unknown name just a year before, was suddenly the talk of Washington, DC. He was called to testify about automobile safety before Congress in February 1966, and his testimony was as thought-provoking and critical as his book. He was not just critical of the auto industry itself; he attacked the entire system that allowed things to get so bad. "A democratic policy," he told Congress, "should not permit an industry to unilaterally decide how many years it wishes to hold back the installation of superior braking systems, safer tires, fuel tanks that do not rupture and incinerate passengers in otherwise survivable accidents, collapsible steering columns, safer instrument panels, steering assemblies, seat structures and frame strengths . . ."

When GM realized that Nader's book was the reason more people were suddenly filing lawsuits against them, they hired a detective agency to follow Nader around and see if they could dig up anything negative about him to help them discredit him, his research, and his book. It was a pretty in-depth and invasive investigation. The detectives dug deep into Nader's past. They went to Nader's childhood town of Winsted. They questioned his childhood and college friends, asking them very personal questions, such as what his grades were like and why he wasn't married yet. Nader was even followed around Washington, DC, where he lived at the time. The detective agency also tried to set him up with women so they could take photos and blackmail him.

In early March 1966, newspapers reported that GM had hired a detective agency to investigate Nader's life in an attempt to discredit Nader and his book. General Motors issued a press release admitting they had hired detectives for a "routine investigation" of Nader, but in fact, it went way beyond that. The president of General Motors, James Roche, was called before Congress on March 22 and was forced to confront how far the detectives had gone. Roche apologized for having Nader investigated. "Let me make clear at the outset that I deplore the kind of harassment to which Mr. Nader has apparently been subjected. I am just as shocked and outraged by some of the incidents which

FROM *UNSAFE AT ANY SPEED* BY RALPH NADER (NEW YORK: BANTAM, 1973) PP 56–57.

WITH EVERY NEW MODEL YEAR, IT MUST BE presumed, on the basis of the evidence dealing with breakdowns in product quality, thousands of drivers are driving defective new cars that are likely to be involved in accidents. Hundreds of dealers know this, but are either obeying company orders or are protecting their own interests by remaining silent.

The 1953 Roadmaster case, the Ford suspension arm, and the Chrysler steering wheel bracket are evidence of breakdown in production quality control. Even more insidious are hazards that are the products of design. Born of deliberate knowledge, these hazards are far less likely to be admitted by car makers when they are confronted with substantial

evidence of their danger. And, of course, motorists are not warned of these hazards in owner's manuals.

The connection between design defects and driver misjudgment or uncontrollable vehicle behavior is so subtle that neither the accident investigator nor the operator is aware of this connection in collisions. Automatic transmission defects illustrate this point with spectacularly tragic consequences. With more and more vehicles employing automatic transmissions, the occurrence of the "engine-powered runaway accident" is rising alarmingly. These accidents display a similar pattern. A vehicle starting from a standstill or at a very low speed careens or lurches completely out of control with startling unexpectancy. For example:

- A young lady enters her garage and gets into her car to go to work. An instant later the car plummets in the wrong direction straight through the back end of the garage.
- A middle-aged woman is maneuvering her car out of a parked position on a busy main street; suddenly, the car shoots forward across the street over the sidewalk and crashes fifty feet through a store window, narrowly missing a number of pedestrians and store clerks.
- An automobile is coming out of a parking garage; abruptly it lurches forward and then careens wildly, killing or injuring pedestrians and patrons of a restaurant.
- A woman shopper is trying to back up her car from a street parking area. The automobile's front wheels are against the curb. On pressing the accelerator to ease out backwards, the vehicle does not respond; the driver presses down further on the gas. The car jumps the curb, crosses an alley to a nearby house and kills a couple sunning themselves in their own backyard.
- A couple drives into a lumber yard. The husband gets out of the car and notices that his wife has stopped three feet short of

a marked area. He asks her to pull up the required distance. She shifts to what she thinks is the forward gear. (The car door is open, and he is guiding her.) The car backs up instead; the open door knocks him down and the car runs over him and kills him.

These are actual cases illustrating the common transmission-induced accidents which trap the driver. They occur because of negligent design of the automatic transmission shift patterns. The driver is charged with reckless driving or negligent manslaughter. Rarely does the police officer recognize that the accident he is investigating proceeded from a built-in design hazard that materialized.

In many instances these "drivers errors" are the result of confusion over the bewildering variety of automatic shifting devices offered in different makes and models of automobiles.

General Motors had detectives follow Ralph Nader because they wanted to discredit his research into their cars.

Mr. Nader has reported as the members of this committee." He continued: "We in General Motors certainly would not want any private citizen to think for one moment that he was not free to criticize our corporation or products, before this subcommittee or anyone else, without fear of retaliation or harassment of any kind."

Partly as a result of the publicity and shocking revelations surrounding the testimony, *Unsafe at Any Speed* became a bestseller and pressured auto makers to do something. The book made Ralph Nader a household name and launched a career fighting against corporate power and promoting stricter government standards. It also gave courage to other people around the country who were thinking of taking a stand against a defective product, and attempting to change the world around them in other ways.

On September 9, 1966, President Johnson signed the Highway Safety Act of 1966 and the National Traffic and Motor Vehicle Safety Act into law. Ralph Nader was there to witness the signing of the bills. Afterward, President Johnson gave him one of the pens used to sign them. Still, change did not come immediately;

seatbelts were still optional in most cars, and though they were standard issue in Cadillacs, if you paid an extra twenty-seven dollars you could have a new car without seatbelts. However, that would soon change—a new automobile safety standard went into effect in 1968 that made seatbelts mandatory in all passenger vehicles.

CHAPTER TWO

UNSAFE!

UNSAFE AT ANY SPEED HAD A HUGE IMPACT ON
the automobile industry. By 1973, twenty-eight
million cars had been recalled for safety issues.
But as Nader pointed out in the revised edition of
the book, since the first publication of *Unsafe at
Any Speed* in 1965, 330,000 more Americans had
died in car accidents and twenty-five million more
had been injured. He added one hundred pages of
new material to the original book to keep making
the case for increased automobile safety.

But cars were not the only things that young
Nader was fighting to improve. There was a lot
out there in the world that was unsafe! He seized
the momentum of the book and started to work
on numerous other causes as well. Over the next

few years, his reputation continued to grow and he developed a following of young people who were inspired by his work. Nader was featured on the cover of *Time* in 1969 with the headline "The Consumer Revolt." The accompanying article referred to Nader as "the nation's toughest customer." It was true; Nader sparked a consumer movement that grew stronger with every passing year. He was present when President Johnson signed the Wholesome Meat Act of 1967, and so was one of his childhood heroes—eighty-nine-year-old Upton Sinclair, who championed improvements to the meat packing industry back in 1906.

Things were looking very positive indeed for the future of consumer protection. But one person can only do so much, no matter how popular they are. Nader knew that it had taken years to work on *Unsafe at Any Speed*. He needed help to accomplish the wide-ranging investigative work on consumer and government issues that would improve people's lives. He needed a team of people, an army of researchers and investigators.

Those people who worked for him and dedicated themselves to the causes he

championed earned the nickname "Nader's
Raiders." When Nader organized the first team
in June 1968, they were mainly law students
who were tasked with investigating and exposing
government agency practices and policies. These
young people did extensive research, conducted
many interviews, and wrote up their findings.
The first report issued by Nader's Raiders was
about the Federal Trade Commission (FTC),
whose purpose was to protect consumers from
defective products. Printed in 1969, the 185-
page report found many problems with the
agency and made recommendations to fix them,
including a call for the resignation of the FTC
chairman Paul Rand Dixon. Having an army of
helpers seemed to be working, so more help was
recruited. In early 1969, an ad in the Harvard
University student newspaper said: "Nader's
Raiders. Graduate students in medicine, biology,
life sciences, engineering, and law are needed
this summer to work with Ralph Nader in an
investigation of various government programs."

There was a surge of interest in joining
the movement. Over the next four years, a
dozen reports were issued by Nader's Raiders,
including a groundbreaking report on the

Some of the reports issued by Nader's Raiders and published in book form.

Food and Drug Administration, called "The Chemical Feast," which focused on the lack of proper regulation of additives in American food products. Another report, "Vanishing Air," focused on air pollution in the United States, while "Water Wasteland" dealt with water pollution. Many of these reports wound up being published as paperback books (with introductions by Nader) that the general public could read and understand. The first four reports sold more than 450,000 copies. They detailed how government agency policies, combined with manufacturer indifference, were allowing harmful pollutants and products to infiltrate daily life and endanger us all.

While he oversaw the research teams, Nader was also busy founding organizations that furthered his goals as a consumer advocate. In 1968, he founded the Center for Study of Responsive Law to serve as his main office in Washington, DC. In 1971, Nader founded the group Public Citizen, whose goals are to "defend democracy, resist corporate power and work to ensure that government works for the people—not for big corporations." Some of the other groups he founded, or helped found over the years, include the Center for Auto Safety, National Consumer Organization, Pension Rights Center, Center for Science in the Public Interest, Citizen Advocacy Center, Clean Water Action Project, Center for Justice and Democracy, Consumer Watchdog, the Disability Rights Center, and numerous university student public interest research groups, or PIRGs, throughout the country.

In creating safe places for people to organize responses to serious consumer issues, Nader helped Americans take control of their lives and their communities. Instead of feeling powerless, they could start to feel influential.

Besides starting organizations dedicated to uncovering truth and helping the average citizen, Nader also pushed for landmark legislation and for the creation of new oversight agencies. His efforts helped create new federal regulatory agencies, such as the Occupational Safety and Health Administration (OSHA), the Environmental Protection Agency (EPA), and the Consumer Product Safety Commission (CPSC). He helped get the Safe Drinking Water Act, the Pure Food and Drug Act, the Clean Air Act, and the 1967 Freedom of Information

Act (FOIA) passed and signed. FOIA is an extremely important law that says citizens have the right to request records from any federal agency, so long as they are not classified or invasions of personal privacy. Understanding what the government is doing, and why, is important. In 2018, the EPA received 11,364 FOIA requests; the Department of Defense received 56,336 requests; the Department of Justice received 96,875 requests; and the Department of Homeland Security received 395,751 requests. The Freedom of Information Act has become so important that people these days use it as a verb: "I don't have the information, so I'm going to FOIA it."

By the early 1970s, Nader's popularity was at a new high. He was rubbing elbows with many famous people. In 1972, he appeared on a television show with John Lennon and Yoko Ono and talked politics and people power. In 1972, Nader was approached by the New Party to run as their candidate for president, but he was not interested. He also got one vote to be the vice-presidential nominee at the 1972 Democratic National Convention. Nader continued to work on consumer rights, but politics would come calling again twenty years later. In 1992, he appeared as a "none of the above" write-in candidate on the Democratic primary ballot in New Hampshire and came in eighth out of forty-seven candidates on the ballot. He was a write-in candidate on the Republican ballot and came in fourth out of fifty candidates—remarkably, about the same number of votes he received from the Democrats. He was also on the ballot in Massachusetts and came in fourth place. In 1996, Nader was drafted to run for president on the Green Party ticket. He appeared on the ballot in just twenty-two states but still got 685,297 votes, or 0.71 percent of the total popular vote.

Encouraged by those results, he remained open to running again. In 2000, the year the major party candidates were George W. Bush (Republican) and Al Gore (Democrat), Nader was officially nominated by the Green Party to run as their candidate for president. He attracted support and endorsements from many celebrities, including the singers Patti Smith and Willie Nelson, television host Phil Donohue, actor Paul Newman, and actress Susan Sarandon.

He attracted a paying crowd of twenty thousand people to a massive Madison Square Garden rally in New York City billed as "Ralph Rocks the Garden." It featured several guest speakers and musical performances from the likes of Eddie Vedder (lead singer of the band Pearl Jam) and the folk-rock singer Ani DiFranco. Why does Nader think were people drawn to him in 2000? "My record of defending people—as consumers, patients, breathers, workers, children," he explains. Nader was different from the major party candidates. His campaign was about "stressing the shift of power from the few to the many," in his words. Those who listened heard an authenticity. He knew what he was talking about and tried to get people to think, instead of simply following party politics and slogans. Because of a strictly controlled two-party system, he was prevented from appearing in the televised debates between the two major candidates. Come Election Day, he came in third place behind George Bush and Al Gore and got 2,883,105 votes, or 2.74 percent of the popular vote. In some states, he did far better; in Alaska, he received 10 percent of the popular vote, and in Vermont, he got 7 percent.

Committed to breaking through the two-party system, Nader ran again in 2004. This time he got 465,650 votes, or 0.38 percent of the popular vote total. He ran again in 2008 as an Independent, and did better, getting 739,034 votes, or 0.56 percent of the popular vote total. Nader considered running again in 2012 but decided against it. Over his four campaigns, he received a total of 4,773,086 votes for president and raised awareness about the need for laws serving the people first, electoral reform, and two-party system reform.

After leaving political office aspirations behind, Nader continued to fight for the American public on many important issues and wrote numerous books. But in March of 2019, a very personal tragedy shook his family and set him on a new drive at the age of eighty-five. Ethiopian Airlines Flight 302 crashed in Ethiopia five minutes after takeoff from Addis Ababa Airport, on its way to Nairobi Airport in Kenya, killing all 157 people on board. One of the passengers happened to be Samya Stumo, Ralph Nader's grandniece, who was an emerging leader in global health. The plane was a Boeing 737 MAX model, new, with only 1,332 hours of flight time. Yet this was the second time in less than a year that this new type of plane had crashed; in October 2018, Lion Air Flight 610, with only nine hundred hours in the air, crashed in Asia. It was no coincidence. The 737 MAX had a problem, and once Nader, the grieving families, the media, and others began to dig deeper, they found a lot of troubling information about the history of the aircraft and a serious lack of engineering safety by its manufacturer, Boeing.

The 737's Maneuvering Characteristics Augmentation Software (MCAS) was found to be the cause of both crashes. The software was created to kick in when the airplane's nose was pointed too high up, which can cause the engines to stall and the plane to crash. The MCAS was supposed to kick in when the angle of the nose reached a critical point, and stabilize the plane before it could stall. The problem in the 737 MAX was the MCAS system took control and did not let the pilots resume control—and if, like in these crashes, the sensors were malfunctioning and the MCAS incorrectly sensed a high nose angle, it would try to angle the plane lower.

In the doomed October 2018 flight, the pilots were in a battle with the MCAS system over control of the plane. Every time the system kicked in, it sent the plane pitching downward. The pilots tried to correct it, but the MCAS kicked in again and angled the plane downward. After many of these intensifying, terrifying up and down movements, the pilots were overpowered by the MCAS. It was too late. The plane crashed into the Java Sea. The events leading to the Ethiopian Airlines crash five months later were similar. Once MCAS engaged, the pilots fought to keep the plane's nose up, but the MCAS ultimately won and the plane crashed.

In the weeks and months after the second crash, there was a growing uproar among the victims' families and airplane safety groups to hold Boeing accountable for the disasters. All the 737 MAX planes were grounded worldwide while Boeing looked into fixing the software. But the 737 MAX was Boeing's fastest-selling model ever, with over five thousand planes ordered by various airlines. Nader appeared in many television and radio interviews calling for Boeing to suspend production of this aircraft. He wanted the Federal Aviation Administration (FAA) to recertify the entire plane, not just the MCAS. Boeing set up a separate page on their website just for updates on the 737 MAX, telling the public that they updated the software, completed more than 1,100 test and production flights, and established a $100 million relief fund "to meet family and community needs of those affected by these accidents."

For Nader, the fight against Boeing was a tragic full circle moment, reminiscent of the giant automaker he had taken on almost fifty-five years earlier. With over 150,000 employees, Boeing is one of the largest and most powerful corporations in the world. In 2018 alone, the company was awarded federal government contracts valued at almost $14 billion. The 737 MAX story is a reminder of why large corporations can be dangerous if left unchecked by weak regulations. Thanks to a combination of publicity about the history of the dangerous MCAS system and a persistent outcry from victims' families and safety officials, Boeing started to take action.

According to Nader, the Boeing tragedies are just more warning signs of things to come; with advanced computers able to do things like drive our cars for us, the potential for deadly accidents is still there. Computers do malfunction, and if the human driver is unable to override in time, the results can be disastrous.

Nader's life work continues to be as relevant now as it was back in 1965 when his first book came out. For example, the 2019 impeachment of President Donald Trump was put into motion when a whistleblower came forward with information about a questionable phone call between President Trump and the newly elected president of Ukraine, Volodymyr Zelensky. Who was it that coined the modern usage of the word "whistleblower"? Ralph Nader. (The term existed before, but it had a negative meaning until Nader spun it in a more positive light and encouraged people of conscience to come forward and reveal harmful business and governmental practices.) And who was it who helped push through Congress the Whistleblower Protection Act of 1989, often referenced in the days after the impeachment investigation was set into motion?

Yes, it was Ralph Nader.

CHAPTER THREE

THE RISE OF CORPORATE IDENTITIES

SO HOW EXACTLY DID WE GET TO WHERE WE are today, where corporations have so much power and control? How did we get to an America where people like Ralph Nader have to fight so hard to empower our citizens to take back their country? It certainly wasn't always like this.

To understand, we need to take a trip back in time to colonial days . . .

Four hundred years ago, you would not have gone far to obtain whatever supplies you needed for your day-to-day life. Every town had a baker, butcher, miller, beer brewer, weaver, carpenter, and blacksmith. Local farms produced milk, eggs, and wool. The wood from local trees was used to build houses and furniture. There were no "companies" or brands, only individuals or families who specialized in a particular trade and served the locals. It was always easier and cheaper to get your necessary items locally. If you had a problem with an item you purchased, you'd take up the issue directly with the seller; you'd literally knock on Jack Johnson's door and tell him the cheese was spoiled. If he did not want to lose you as a customer, he'd make it right and offer you your money back or a fresh hunk of cheese instead.

Most disputes were between equals. Since everything was localized, business owners did not have more "power" than anyone else, because almost everyone was involved in one business or another—making candles, milling flour, butchering meat, weaving linen, or carving furniture. If you made flour you relied on the candlemaker to light your home, and he relied on your flour to make his meals.

By the early nineteenth century, you could still get whatever food or supplies you needed from a handful of local merchants. You had a one-on-one relationship with these folks, and they usually dealt directly with the suppliers of the raw materials and foodstuffs. But things were starting to change. The population of the newly independent country was growing fast, and people were settling further west, staking out new territory.

Some of the earliest companies with widely distributed foods, such as alcohol, tea, and chocolate, were products that did not need special preservation, treatment, or technology to stay fresh. For example, Caswell-Massey (founded in 1752) made soap and perfume, King Arthur (1790) made flour, and Jim Beam (1795) made whiskey. In those days there were no airplanes, automobiles, or trains, so anything that was sent from one place to another was either sent by ship and/or by horse and wagon.

The completion of the Erie Canal in 1825 was a major step in helping goods get around the country. You could have a manufacturing operation in New York City and send your products quickly and easily via water all the way to the Midwest. The invention of the railroad just after the canal opened, and the subsequent laying of tracks all across the country, made it even easier to ship products greater distances.

Transportation was not the only advancement. As the nineteenth century progressed, the Industrial Revolution's more efficient machines led to better food processing technology, allowing people to start companies that made large quantities of products to sell to more people in more places. Everything from the way crops were harvested to the way food was produced started to rely on machines. But why would an average baker, who made a living selling cakes to the locals, want to create a company, hire many employees, and start delivering cakes elsewhere?

The motivation for creating companies was simple: profit and prestige. Small scale success was nice—but why not be even more successful? The more cakes made and sold, the more profit could be made. The more profit made, the bigger the company could get—expanding to new areas and selling more cakes and making more profits. With technology, cakes could be made by the thousands. There were still local bakers with a few employees, but there were also large baking companies with hundreds of employees. Some companies tried but failed to grow bigger with success. Maybe their products were not so great; maybe they lost too much money. Others sold well and were able to grow, thanks in part to the ever-expanding railroad. By 1850, there were 9,000 miles of railroad track in the country; by 1860, the number was 30,000 miles. By 1916, it was over 250,000 miles of track.

Railroad Companies

It took a lot of work to get railroad service across the nation. Laying track was not simple. The path the tracks would follow had to be cleared and materials brought to the site. Workers had to place wooden ties, drive the spikes, lay the gravel in the rail bed, and measure and calculate to make sure everything was straight and done right. Railroad companies like Union Pacific (founded 1862) had to hire thousands of workers to keep the tracks going. In Bald Knob, Arkansas, for example, railroad officials discovered local rocks that would work well for rail bed ballast. They opened a rock quarry in 1877, and more than a quarter of the townspeople wound up working there. In June 1868, Julesburg, Colorado, was a brand-new railroad town with forty-one residents. By the end of July the population grew to four

THE GREAT RACE FOR THE WESTERN STAKES 1870

By 1870, railroads were already among the most powerful companies in the country.

thousand, thanks to the Union Pacific Railroad, which sold town lots at a thousand dollars each.

Railroad work could be very intense, and it was not just about the tracks. Sometimes obstacles were in the way. Near Truckee, California, work crews spent two years boring a 1,659-foot-long tunnel (less than a third of a mile) through the Sierra Nevada mountain range at Donner Summit.

As tracks were laid, many people came to the site to get work. After the tracks were finished and train service was introduced, there were still many people in these railroad towns who were employed by the railroads—everything from kids sweeping rail depot floors to stationmasters and machinists. Plenty of towns in the west were founded simply because of the railroad's presence. Existing settlements turned from quiet little places to growing, thriving towns.

Railroads were a dangerous business for the rail workers. In those days the rail cars had to be coupled together by hand; the links connected while one car was pushed into position with the other. Many workers were injured or even killed in coupling accidents. In 1892 alone, there were eleven thousand casualties (injuries or deaths) related to coupling accidents.

The railroad companies were among the first really big companies in the country. They controlled vast amounts of wealth because their rails carried trains laden with goods heading to every corner of the United States. The railroads also played an important role in helping other companies grow by allowing their products to be shipped far and wide.

Even with the invention of cars and planes, railroads still play a huge role moving goods and people around the country. The Union Pacific Railroad still exists and has 32,200 miles of track, 42,000 employees, and spends $3.2 billion a year. The old folk song "I've Been Working on the Railroad" is a popular leftover of the days when the railroad was king.

Coal Towns

Developing alongside the railroads were coal mines. Coal mining, unlike railroad work, was stationary. You needed to live near the mine if you worked there, and mining companies often built housing for their workers. Coal mining companies opened stores in which the miners could shop for their daily needs, because these coal mines might be located in newly built towns on isolated land owned by the mining company. Workers paid in cash except when they were short on money and needed an advance on their paycheck. The mining company would give them an advance in the form of "scrip," which was the credit card of the day. Some mining operations only paid their employees in scrip and not cash. Miners could shop using the scrip, but it was only good at the company store. The miners could sell their scrip to a middleman for cash if they were desperate, but they'd only get around seventy-five cents for every dollar. Other stores began to accept scrip for payment, but they discounted it heavily, so if you wanted to buy something that cost a dollar you might have to use one dollar and fifty cents worth of scrip. It was an unfair system but the miners were stuck. It was easy to get into debt if you needed or wanted merchandise, everything from chewing gum to toys to mining equipment. Many miners felt that they owed their souls to the company store because of the way the system worked.

In 1945, the United States Supreme Court heard a case brought by mine workers against their employer, the Jewell Ridge Coal Corporation in Virginia. The miners were being paid the moment they arrived at the coal mining work site—but they believed they should be on the clock when they entered the main mine portal. The Court ruled in their favor, stating in the majority opinion that miners "are unlike the ordinary traveler or the ordinary workman on his way to work. They must journey beneath the crust of the earth, far removed from the fresh and open air and from the beneficial rays of the sun. A heavy toll is exacted from those whose lot it is to ride and walk and mine beneath the surface. From the moment they enter the portal until they leave, they are subjected to constant hazards and danger." This danger remains even now, and coal miners work under threat of disaster that could injure or kill them.

Even into the twenty-first century, coal mining remains a major component of American energy production, providing around 50 percent of the country's energy. As of 2017, there were still fifty-three thousand people employed in coal mines in the United States. The leading producer of American coal, Peabody Energy, is the largest coal company in the world.

Coal was not the only valuable natural resource—silver, gold, iron, and copper were all mined in the nineteenth century, often by large and powerful companies.

The Rise of the Corporation

By the late nineteenth century, corporations were becoming larger, more powerful, and more present in everyday life. You could still shop in your own town, but now you'd find boxed and canned products made by big companies on the shelves alongside things that were made locally. Mass production required factories, and factories required hundreds or thousands of workers. A growing percentage of the population now relied on large corporations for their existence, often under harsh working conditions. Because mass-produced products might be cheaper than the local versions, they began to threaten the existence of the small local store. Companies like Sears (starting in 1888) began selling mass-produced items through the mail using catalogs, shipping them anywhere in the country.

There had always been wealthy people in the US, but it was during the late nineteenth century that a new class of wealthy began to emerge.

These were the super wealthy, people who had massive amounts of money. One of the first such families was the Vanderbilts, who made their fortune on railroads and shipping. It was a Vanderbilt who was responsible for building Grand Central Terminal in New York City, and a Vanderbilt who created the country's first modern highway. Andrew Carnegie founded the Carnegie Steel Company and became one of the richest people in the country. Carnegie sold the company in 1901 to the super wealthy J.P. Morgan, and it became US Steel. In the early twentieth century, automobile makers began turning to mass production, allowing them to grow their operations tremendously. Ford Motor Company made nineteen thousand cars in 1910. By 1916, that number increased to five hundred thousand.

As the years passed, car companies grew from small operations into some of the biggest corporations in the country. It was now possible to mass produce almost anything using ores that were extracted from the ground, trees that were more efficiently cut and processed, and other materials that were refined with automation. New food packaging technology helped create

A 1900 political cartoon about Andrew Carnegie.

longer lasting products. More and more products appeared on the shelves with brand names made by companies that churned out countless thousands of cans, boxes, and jars of food items. With the growing network of railroad tracks across the United States and the advent of cars and trucks, manufacturers were able to ship their products far and wide. Mail order catalogs became popular, offering anyone, anywhere in the country, a wide range of mass-produced products. Sears, Roebuck and Company even offered complete home kits for sale; they shipped the kit, and you assembled the house.

As corporate power grew, so too did injuries and deaths of workers in all kinds of industries, where safety was not a major concern—not when profit was at stake. From meatpacking to automobile assembly lines, workers died and were injured by the thousands. Their pain and suffering eventually led to the rise of the labor movement and to worker protection laws—and also to the evolution of tort law, as we'll see later in this book.

CHAPTER FOUR

CORPORATIONS TODAY

MANY OF TODAY'S FAMOUS BRANDS STARTED out as small businesses over a hundred years ago, serving local customers only, and then growing bigger and bigger over time. For example, Entenmann's started out in 1898 as a small bakery in Brooklyn, New York, and during the twentieth century grew to become a nationwide name. By the middle of the twentieth century, not only were there lots of really big and powerful corporations, these corporations began to merge with each other at a rapid pace to create even larger companies. Most of the food brands you see in the stores today used to be made by independent companies. Things like Tropicana orange juice, Entenmann's cakes, and 7Up soda were once independently run brands. Over the years, these brands were bought by other brands that were bought by bigger brands. Today there are super companies, many of them multinational, consisting of a collection of companies from different countries. Some companies resisted the urge to merge and faded away soon after. The author's great-grandfather, as the story goes, rejected an offer by Best Foods to purchase the family's successful New York City horseradish operation. Soon after, the business was finished.

There were thousands of small and medium-sized companies that flourished during the early and mid-twentieth century. Some companies grew at a faster rate than others, and became really large, with worldwide distribution. These companies wanted to continue to grow, and the only way to do that was to expand their product line. Rather than try to enter the market for, say, donuts—a market already crowded with well-known and trusted donut brands—larger companies bought smaller ones and created a family of brands that they controlled. As of 2020, PepsiCo, the maker of Pepsi soft drinks, owned

Fritos, Doritos, Cheetos, Aunt Jemima, Lay's, Quaker, and Rice-A-Roni, among others. What about Entenmann's? In 1978, it was bought by a pharmaceutical company, then in 1982, it was bought by General Foods (which later merged with Kraft). A few owners later and Entenmann's was sold to a large Mexican company called Grupo Bimbo, which also owns Sara Lee and Thomas'. Take a careful look at the fine print on some of the food containers on your shelves or in your fridge. That famous brand you know and love may well turn out to be owned by a much larger company.

This merging trend is not just present in the food industry. It's pretty much a trend for any kind of major company. In the book publishing world, what used to be many independent publishers are now a few major companies that own several "brands," which used to be their own companies. Penguin Random House, for example, is described on its Wikipedia page as an "American multi-national conglomerate publishing company." Sounds scary, right? It's a long way from the days in the eighteenth century when Benjamin Franklin published books in Philadelphia.

The Walt Disney Company was plenty large and powerful by the mid-twentieth century, but now it also owns the television network ABC, as well as the TV studio 20th Television (formerly 20th Century Fox TV). ViacomCBS owns the CBS network, Paramount Pictures, MTV, Nickelodeon, and Simon & Schuster publishing. Large corporations often amass a collection of companies that are not even in the same industry. For example, Berkshire Hathaway owns GEICO (insurance), Dairy Queen (ice cream), Fruit of the Loom (underwear), Duracell (batteries), and Pampered Chef (cookware).

When companies focusing on one type of product or service become so large that they buy out practically all the competition, this creates a monopoly. A monopoly can therefore control the prices of that product or service. The wealthy John D. Rockefeller had one of the country's first monopolies. He bought numerous oil refineries until he controlled 90 percent of all the oil business in the country in the late nineteenth century. Soon, the sugar and rubber industries were also controlled by monopolies. In 1890, Congress passed the Sherman Antitrust Act to try to limit the corporate takeover of entire industries, but monopolies are still a problem to this day.

Companies today can grow really large and have business all over the world. JP Morgan Chase, for example, is worth more than $368 billion and has over 250,000 employees, according to *Forbes*'s list of the world's largest public companies. But they pale in comparison to the Industrial and Commercial Bank of China, which has almost 450,000 employees; China National Petroleum, which has over 1.3 million employees; and Walmart, with its 2.2 million employees.

Corporate Power

What does all this mean to the consumer? Are these gigantic corporations good or bad for us? While mass production or wholesale buying power that giant companies offer can reduce the prices we pay (as is true of Walmart, for example), overall, corporations are not good for us.

Corporations distance us from the products we buy. No longer can you go down to the person who sold the pancake flour with worms in it. Now you have to call a consumer hotline and likely talk to someone in another country in a call center filled with people who are hired to handle consumer complaints for a variety of companies. You're about as far away from the people who made the product as you can be. And you are just one voice out of millions of customers. In the old days, you might be one voice out of fifty customers, which was important enough that you'd be listened to. If you told your friends and family not to go to that flour mill anymore, they could lose their customers just like that. It was in their interest to keep people happy. It's true that social media gives a voice to those who complain, but it's still a drop in the bucket in the face of a large corporation. So, you may receive a coupon in the mail to replace the defective product—but will your concerns and similar ones by many other customers really be heard and dealt with? Outside the company, who knows?

Product defects, though, can be much worse than just a moldy package of cheese—remember the defective cars in chapter 1? Corporations want to make money—lots of it—and sometimes, product quality and safety are sacrificed in the name of making a profit. Sometimes companies know their products are faulty and don't do anything to fix them. And that can be a very dangerous problem.

The larger the company, the more "faceless" it can appear. Contacting such companies (not a hotline, the actual company) can be difficult; talking to a real person can be a challenge, especially in this internet era. There are obviously people behind such giants as Amazon, but you have to go through a maze to speak to a human (if you can even get that far) when you have an issue. And when you do get someone on the phone, chances are they are not sitting in the corporate headquarters in the United States but are a citizen of another faraway country, like India or the Philippines, working in a call center to handle customer service for the American company that hired them. Modern technology has been great for helping companies get their message and product to consumers on a daily basis, but it's made them more remote from you than ever before.

It's not just the customers of a large company who are affected. The average person anywhere, who may never even buy the product, is affected. The bigger a company, the more power they have to influence politics and policies that touch us all. Companies have money and money buys influence.

A company that employs ten thousand people in one state could have more influence on the politicians you elect than one that employs just one hundred people. Those ten thousand people represent jobs and money in the local economy, and the politicians know that. The company can try to use that as leverage to get special deals, like tax breaks from the government, to stay put instead of leaving for another location.

Corporate Lobbying

Large companies donate massive amounts of money to the campaigns of politicians running for office. They also lobby the politicians who are currently in Congress for favors. They spend a fortune—and hope to get back much more than that. In 2018, the insurance company Blue Cross Blue Shield spent more than $23 million lobbying politicians in Washington, DC, alone. Why would insurance companies want to lobby Washington, DC? Like any company—to preserve profits and keep growing. If a plan like "Medicare for All" became law, that would give the federal government more control over health care and reduce the power of insurance companies.

With a system that would give free health care to more people, insurance companies' profits (and their very existence) could be threatened. Doctors could also be threatened, since they would not be able to charge as much for their services. Drug companies also spend a fortune lobbying Washington, DC; according to the Center for Responsive Politics, more than four hundred clients spent $228 million to have 1,400 lobbyists try to influence Congress in 2018. Why? Simple: to keep the cost of the prescription drugs they make high and fight against measures that would seek to lower drug prices.

What kind of political favors are worth that much money to anyone? Usually, these favors come in the form of the laws that Congress passes. Laws can impact corporations or groups of people (like doctors or gun owners) in major ways. They can hurt or help companies. They can hurt or help certain groups of people. The lobbyists that try to influence Congress want to make sure the laws that are passed will benefit them and their clients.

A railroad lobbyist depicted in a 1902 political cartoon.

Sometimes, large companies, or their supporters, band together to form organizations. Groups like the National Rifle Association (NRA, 5,000,000 members) and the American Medical Association (AMA, 250,000 members) are also very powerful because of the size of their membership.

In just the first six months of 2019, the NRA spent $1.6 million lobbying against a proposed law that would mandate stricter background checks for people trying to buy guns. Why would the NRA care about background checks, which seems like a generally good idea? For two reasons—background checks would eliminate a percentage of gun sales to those people, and the very idea of a background check would discourage others from buying guns. Bottom line is that the gun makers would lose business, and the NRA would have unhappy members who would feel like their organization did not accomplish its goal.

The AMA spent more than $21 million on lobbying for their members (which includes many thousands of doctors) in 2018. Why would they spend so much—and for what? To protect doctors' incomes.

Corporate lobbying is always about protecting a group's interests, weakening law enforcement, and keeping profits flowing. Let's say there is an environmental regulation currently in effect that forces certain companies to spend a lot of money to clean up toxic chemicals that are created when they make their products. The companies, through a lobbying firm, might try to get Congress to repeal or weaken that legislation or reduce the agency's budget. While corporations themselves aren't allowed to give donations to politicians, the lobbyists they hire are allowed to set up fund-raisers for the congresspeople, where each guest might pay $1,000 for dinner and a chance to meet the politician.

Let's say Jack is a one-term senator and he is up for re-election. He will need lots of cash to run his campaign. If a fund-raiser created by a plastics company helps him and raises a million dollars for him, it will be hard to ignore them when the plastics company asks for his support in repealing that law. But it takes more than one vote in Congress to enact or repeal a law, so corporations that want to push their agenda have to target the right people, the ones who are not decided and could make a difference in the vote.

They might not waste their time on politicians who have spoken out strongly against changing the toxic chemical law, or maybe on those who have spoken out strongly in favor of changing the law either. Sometimes, it's actually former members of Congress who turn into lobbyists; they are attractive to corporations because they already know the ins and outs of Congress.

The kinds of legislation that large corporations lobby against can be hard to believe at first glance. Why would anyone spend millions of dollars to oppose a national wind production tax credit that gives incentives to people who harness wind power to create energy, something that's good for the environment and the future of the planet? Because it threatens oil and gas industry profits. Corporations also exert their influence to get tax laws to work in their favor, allowing them to avoid paying taxes while the average person struggling to make ends meet is stuck paying a hefty part of their income.

Isn't it true that everyone has the right to have their voice heard and let Congress know what they think? It is, but wealthy corporations have an unfair advantage, because their voice is heard with money and power. The corporate breaks that large companies receive mainly benefit the people who manage and own the company, not the millions of workers who may earn very little money no matter how much good fortune the company has. Walmart employs 1.5 million people in the US; according to the Center for Responsive Politics, the company spent $6.1 million using sixty lobbyists to lobby the government for laws favorable to its business in 2019. Meanwhile, there have been a variety of serious complaints about how the huge company (which earns billions of dollars in profits every year) treats its workers.

Individual people can donate money to a politician, but that money does not come with an attached viewpoint. With lobbyist money it's very clear where the group behind the money stands. If a lobbyist can get a politician on their side and help them win an election, that means two more years (House of Representatives) or six more years (Senate) that the group will have that congressperson on their side.

When billionaire businessman and former New York City mayor Michael Bloomberg ran for president in 2020, he self-funded his campaign and proclaimed he was beholden to no lobbies or special interests because he was not accepting any donations from anyone. Nobody could influence him, he said. Still, some felt that he was his own special interest group because he was contributing money to certain groups and people to get them on his side—a kind of reverse lobbying. Even if nobody could influence him, he could influence them with his money.

Still, even the biggest corporations and their founders or owners can do good. People like Bill Gates, the founder of Microsoft, and his wife Melinda, donate massive amounts of money to charity. They have given more than $36 billion of their fortune. Bloomberg founded Everytown for Gun Safety in 2013 to fight the powerful gun lobby and help push tougher gun safety laws. He also opposed tobacco companies and supported auto safety regulations.

One thing is very clear no matter what your point of view—large corporations, big money, and the people behind that big money have too much power and control too much of what goes on in today's America. And this leaves the average citizen feeling like they have less control and less say in the country's future than ever before.

As of 2019, the top 1 percent of the richest families in America controlled 34.4 percent of the wealth, according to a government report. Meanwhile, the lowest 50 percent of income earners made up only 1.8 percent of the country's wealth. The bottom 90 percent only controlled 30.6 percent of the country's money. America is a country controlled by the super wealthy and the companies they own. The business numbers are even more stark. The top 1 percent of the wealthiest people control 57.5 percent of the business wealth in the country. That means this 1 percent is controlling the biggest and most powerful companies in the country.

Corporate Secrecy

Many corporations operate in near total secrecy. They do not share their product development research or studies about products they market. As Ralph Nader said in Senate testimony in the 1960s, "Without the ability to deny the government, the small businessman, and the ordinary citizen literally every kind and form of information about their activities, large business

Corporate secrecy often means product safety is not prioritized.

enterprises simply could not dominate . . . our political and economic life."

Large corporations sell us most of the products and services we use, and we have too little control over what they make, how they make them, and how much they charge for them. The modern citizen is shackled to the whims of corporations that decide what we eat, drink, wear, and drive. And like what happened with the Corvair and other cars since then, sometimes secrecy covers corporate greed and/or incompetence that can cause many people to suffer terribly.

CHAPTER FIVE

WHAT ARE TORTS AND TORT LAW?

IN TODAY'S WORLD, THERE ARE SO MANY corporations all around us, secretive in their business yet deeply involved in every aspect of our daily lives from the moment we wake up to our smartphone alarm to the moment we go to bed and ask a device to turn off the lights for us. From the internet providers we rely on to the search engines and social media sites we use; from the cable companies through which we watch television shows created by media giants to the books we read published by large multinational companies; from the restaurant chains where we eat to the wholesale clubs and big box stores where we shop for everything from bananas to toilet paper—hardly a minute of our lives goes by without some influence by huge, powerful corporations. Even when we go to the doctor, our visit is covered by an insurance company that might have millions of customers, and even our doctor may work for a large hospital that is part of a group of hospitals. When we get into a car, train, or airplane, we are in vehicles that were built by massive companies. When we go to the gas station, we're using fuel that was refined by an immense, international oil company.

In the old days, there were only a few people who could cause you harm—the circle of people you dealt with every day; your neighbors and fellow merchants. You knew these people; you could go face to face with them. Back then, you knew right away when you were being hurt. These days, we deal with so many more entities, and most of them are large, powerful, faceless corporations who can hurt us with products that are defective or filled with invisible, illness-causing chemicals that can take years to affect us. Our lives today are plagued by wrongs done to us in ways that are often less obvious and harder to pinpoint.

When we have a problem with any of these aspects of our lives, we might think that it's not so simple to deal with the issue because large companies are so powerful and anonymous.

Luckily, the Constitution gives everyone the right to a trial by jury when there is a wrong done to us, no matter where we live or who we are—rich or poor, young or old, regardless of race, religion, or anything else. We are all just people, but in one place we are equals with even the largest companies—in the courtroom.

According to the Seventh Amendment of the Constitution:

> *In suits at common law, where the value in controversy shall exceed twenty dollars, the right of trial by jury shall be preserved, and no fact tried by a jury, shall be otherwise reexamined in any court of the United States, than according to the rules of the common law.*

The Constitution protects our right to a trial by jury, whether it is a criminal or civil case. But the right to have a trial by jury was not a new concept. In fact, our Founding Fathers were continuing a tradition that existed in English common law long before the first colonist ever landed in America.

What is the importance of a jury? Well, think of it this way: if all legal cases were decided by judges, then there would only be a single person deciding the fate of each case—a trained judge with a background in the law, not at all your equal. A jury means that a group of average, randomly picked people get to decide your case, with the oversight of a judge to make sure the proceedings are fair and proper.

The separation of criminal law from civil law goes back hundreds of years. In medieval England, someone found guilty for wronging another person would have to pay a fine to the wronged person and to the crown as well. In those days, the primary concern was whether you were disturbing the "king's peace." All it took was one step onto someone else's land, for example, to be disturbing the king's peace— thus, you were really offending the government and not just the person onto whose land you stepped.

For a hundred years after the Norman conquest of England in 1066, property disputes were settled by battle. The two parties would literally battle each other (sometimes through hired warriors) until one person surrendered or was injured or killed. By the time of King Henry II, who ruled from 1154 to 1189, case defendants could buy the right to have procedural questions decided by the local people, for example if they were too injured or too old to do battle. By the year 1250, this had evolved into being allowed to settle the entire legal issue through trial by juries, instead of through battle, and without having to pay for the privilege of a jury. These juries were not exactly what we think of as juries today; back then, they were more often character witnesses who could say something either positive or negative about whether the person was guilty of the alleged wrongdoing.

What Are Torts?

The two main types of law are criminal law and civil law. Criminal law deals with crimes, or behaviors that the government deems as being harmful to society (think back to the idea of the "king's peace" in old England). The goal of criminal law is to punish a criminal for behavior bad enough to warrant imprisonment—whether it is robbery, assault, or murder.

Civil law, in turn, has two main branches: contract law and tort law. Contract law deals with conflict between two parties who enter into a contract with each other. This could be anything from a movie contract to a real estate contract and can involve individuals or companies. Tort law can also involve individuals or companies, but it deals with "torts." The word "tort" is French for "wrong," and tort law is all about determining when someone has been wronged. Tort law has evolved over the years, but the main principle remains—the constitutional right to a trial by jury for everyone who believes they have been wronged.

There are three main kinds of torts: 1) Intentional, 2) Negligent, and 3) Reckless.

Intentional means a wrong was done on purpose. This kind of tort is usually the easiest to determine and prove. If your ex-friend makes up terrible lies about you and spreads them over the internet, that's an intentional tort. If someone sells you a fake Picasso artwork that they painted themselves, that's intentional. If someone walks up to you and punches you in the face, that's intentional. Just because a tort is intentional does not guarantee the plaintiff will win the case—it still has to be proved with a preponderance (or overwhelming amount) of evidence to a jury.

Negligent means careless, and it is quite possible to be injured because of someone else's carelessness. In this time of distractions, this type of tort is more common than ever. People getting distracted by texting while walking or driving can result in injury to others. Even if you're not distracted it can still result in negligent behavior. Let's say you are carrying a big shovel on your shoulder on a busy sidewalk, and you turn suddenly and smack someone in the head. Tort law says that negligence is no excuse, and if you are injured through someone else's carelessness, you may be able to file a lawsuit. There is a more severe variety of negligence called Gross Negligence, which is worse than negligence though not as bad as recklessness. This is worse than just being foolishly careless—it is consciously acting careless in a way likely to cause an injury. One example would be if a worker knows they should clean up a spill but decides to wait until the next day to do it— then someone slips and falls.

Reckless behavior may not intend to harm anybody, but it is so wild and crazy that there is a good chance someone will get hurt. Drag racing on the wrong side of the road is one example. The driver may not intend to hurt anyone, but the behavior is dangerous and likely to cause an accident. Reckless endangerment can also be a criminal offense, punishable by jail time.

Though these are three different kinds of torts with different degrees of awareness, that does not mean they always result in different degrees of harm or monetary awards (damages). In some cases, negligence and recklessness are easier to prove than in others. Defendants might claim that it was not their fault—that it was the victim who should have been more careful.

One interesting thing to note is that in the eyes of the law, a corporation is considered as a "person" and enjoys something called "corporate personhood" that gives it some of the rights of an actual person. The problem is that this corporate "person" cannot be thrown into jail for wrongdoing, so tort law really is the best way to make sure corporations do not get away with injustices.

The scales of justice in a tort case have to weigh who is at fault.

JARTS
MISSILE GAME
PATENT NO. 2,816,042

FROM THE WEBSITE OF THE AMERICAN MUSEUM OF TORT LAW:

STRICT LIABILITY

STRICT, OR "ABSOLUTE," LIABILITY APPLIES to cases where responsibility for an injury can be imposed on the wrongdoer without proof of negligence or direct fault. What matters is that an action occurred and resulted in the eventual injury of another person.

Defective product cases are prime examples of when liability is maintained despite intent. In lawsuits such as these, the injured consumer only has to establish that their injuries were directly caused by the product in question in order to have the law on their side. The fact that the company did not "intend" for the consumer to be injured is not a factor.

A manufacturer is strictly liable in tort when an article he places on the market, knowing that it is to be used without inspection for defects, proves to have a defect that causes injury to a human being.

The purpose of such liability is to insure that the costs of injuries resulting from defective products are borne by the manufacturers that put such products on the market rather than by the injured persons who are powerless to protect themselves.

A plaintiff suing under a theory of strict liability will need to show that there was a defect, that the defect actually and proximately caused the plaintiff's injury, and that the defect made the product unreasonably dangerous. Not only buyers of the product, but also bystanders or guests and others who do not have a direct relationship with the product can sue for strict liability if they are injured by the product.

EXAMPLES OF STRICT LIABILITY TORTS

Defective products (Product Liability)

Animal attacks (dog bite lawsuits)

Abnormally dangerous activities

(Here's a riddle for you: Who can knowingly, deliberately, and intentionally injure someone, and is not wrongful? Answer: A surgeon. If she does the right operation, in the right way, on the right patient, with the patient's permission, she can deliberately injure the patient—like amputate a limb—but the injury is not wrongful.)

The Many Kinds of Tort Cases

Tort lawsuits range from commonplace injuries to bizarre freak accidents. They cover everything from sudden accidents to illnesses caused by years of exposure to a harmful product. There are torts that cover physical injury (faulty products), and torts that pertain to emotional or character injury (defamation or slander). Below are a few examples of different types of torts.

MEDICAL MALPRACTICE

It's shocking to think that up to 225,000 people die each year in the United States due to some kind of medical malpractice. It is the third leading cause of death, behind heart disease and cancer! Beyond that are thousands more victims who survive but with injuries. But only about 3 percent of medical malpractice victims file lawsuits. So, what exactly is medical malpractice? What can cause it? There can be a wide variety of mistakes and issues, ranging from prescribing the wrong dosage of prescription medication to an unsafe drug or prescribing medication when none is needed. Mistakes during surgery (blatant mistakes such as removing the wrong body part or smaller mistakes such as improper wound closure leading to infection), mistaken diagnosis of an illness, and mistaken treatment of a correctly diagnosed illness are a few more examples. In 2006, a Florida jury awarded $216 million to a misdiagnosed patient who was experiencing stroke symptoms and had told ER nurses about a family history of strokes but was treated for sinusitis and wound up in a coma for three months. New health care concerns were voiced in a *Washington Post* article in July 2020 that exposed a growing crisis in college campus medical care where mistakes can be hazardous to student health, and the challenges of campus care in the era of Covid-19.

DANGEROUS PRODUCTS

Many thousands of tort lawsuits are about dangerous products. In these cases, the manufacturer is usually sued for negligence— either they were careless and let dangerous products into the marketplace, or they did so intentionally, knowing the products were dangerous. These types of cases cover a wide range of products, everything from cigarettes to automobiles, from household appliances to factory equipment, from baby powder to lawn darts. Some products may only injure a few people while others injure thousands.

SPORTS TORTS

By their very nature, sports can be dangerous. If you twist an ankle while swinging a bat or sprain your elbow playing tennis, it's hard to sue anyone. But some sports injuries are more insidious and traumatic. One of the biggest sports tort cases in history was a suit brought against the National Football League (NFL) by 4,500 former players over the lack of proper concern and care for head injuries during play. Some of the retired players suffered from Alzheimer's disease, dementia, depression, and other conditions they blamed on head injuries received during their playing days. So where is the tort here? The players alleged that the NFL concealed the seriousness of their injuries and rushed them back onto the field to play more instead of letting them recover. In 2013, the NFL agreed to pay $765 million to settle the case—a sum many retired players believe is inadequate. Some sports torts are not even related to the game itself. In 2019, a New York Mets fan filed a suit against the team when a T-shirt cannon at Citi Field misfired and a shirt hit him in the face, causing him to suffer a concussion and eye trauma.

SLIP AND FALL

One of the most common torts, slip and fall cases are pretty straightforward on the surface. Someone falls, blames someone else (often a store), and files a suit. These cases can be subjective. What caused the fall? Who was really at fault? As of 2017, Russell J. Kendzior had been an expert witness on more than 750 slip and fall cases and wrote a book called *Floored! Real Life Stories from a Slip and Fall Expert Witness.* The cases he discusses range from ordinary supermarket slips to more unusual cases—for example, one Illinois woman fell during her husband's funeral and hit her head on his casket.

Anyone Can Sue . . . Almost

Everyone has the right to file a tort lawsuit, but one thing you need to have is a legitimate interest in the case. You need to have legal *standing.* You can't file a lawsuit over faulty brakes on X Brand car if you don't have one and never did. You have to have been harmed or have some connection to a harmed party or represent a harmed party to be able to file a suit. The exception to the above example would be if you were injured by the driver of an X Brand car with faulty brakes—then you'd have legal standing to sue. Courts have the authority to dismiss lawsuits that do not meet certain legal standards. In 2020, a federal appeals court ruled that 215 senators and congresspeople who sued President Trump claiming he violated the Foreign Emoluments Clause of the Constitution (which says federal officials cannot receive various kinds of payments from foreign governments) had no legal standing to do so because they were not a majority of Congress.

Exhibit of dangerous toys at the American Museum of Tort Law

CHAPTER SIX

HOW DOES A TORT LAW TRIAL WORK?

CONSIDER THE FOLLOWING SCENARIO: LUCY Jones is badly injured by what she claims is a faulty lawn mower. She can't use her right hand for months, and she wants to sue the manufacturer. She meets with a lawyer, Kate Jackson, and explains what happened. Jackson tells her she can take the case, and there's a good chance of winning. Because she's confident she will win, Jackson agrees to take the case on a contingency basis, meaning she will only get paid for more than her expenses if she wins the case. Jones gathers the documents Jackson will need—the X-rays of her finger, the hospital bill, and the receipt for the lawn mower showing it was only six months old at the time of the accident. Jackson talks to Jones's son, who was there when the accident happened. Jackson also contacts the company that made the mower and serves them with the legal papers. It turns out there are several other reports of people being injured by these lawn mowers around the country, but so far, nobody has filed a lawsuit.

If the defendant (in this case, the manufacturer) believes there is no legitimate grounds for the lawsuit, or that the papers were not served correctly, or even that they are not the right party to be sued, then they can file a *motion to dismiss*. This is a request for a judge to dismiss the entire case before it proceeds any further.

If no such motion is filed or such a motion is filed and rejected, next comes the discovery phase. This is when the attorneys for both sides try to gather evidence and testimony from witnesses. The plaintiff's lawyer (Kate Jackson) requests all relevant documents from the defendant. The lawyers take depositions from both sides, or sworn question and answer statements. It is possible at this point that the defendant's lawyer, Jimmy Johnson, will offer to settle the case out of court. If not, both sides prepare for a trial. A date is set in the court calendar. Jurors are selected. The two sides take turns presenting their opening arguments and calling their witnesses. Both sides get a chance to cross-examine those witnesses, meaning if the president of the mower company, Bobby Jacobs, testifies as a witness for the defense, then Lucy's lawyer can also ask him questions. Here is an example of how questioning might go for both sides.

> *Johnson: Mr. Jacobs, were you aware of any issues with this lawn mower's safety?*
>
> *Jacobs: No. None. This was the first I have heard of any problems with this model.*
>
> *Johnson: Thank you. No further questions.*
>
> *Jackson: Mr. Jacobs, have you seen this news article from the City Times dated five years ago? Your honor, permission to enter this into evidence as Exhibit A.*
>
> *Judge: Permission granted.*
>
> *Jacobs: Now that you hold it up, I remember it.*
>
> *Jackson: And doesn't this article have a quote from you about the problems with this mower?*

Jacobs: I think so, yes.

Jackson: No further questions for this witness.

Conversely, Johnson will want to try to poke holes in Jackson's arguments. For example:

Jackson: So, to recap what happened: you leaned down to turn off the mower and a piece of a stick flew out and mangled your finger?

Jones: That's correct.

Jackson: Thank you. No further questions.

Johnson: Were you holding your phone at the time of the accident?

Jones: Umm. No.

Johnson: I have a deposition from your neighbor across the street who says you were looking at your phone while using the mower. And when asked if you were holding a phone, your son first claimed he couldn't remember, then he said no, then he said he wasn't looking.

After all the witnesses have been called, closing arguments are made by each side. Once that is done, the jury has to decide the outcome of the case and the amount of any monetary award. The award amount is subject to the judge's final discretion and any laws in that state regarding civil case damage limits. The judge may reduce the award amount substantially (by 75 percent or more) if he or she does not feel the evidence presented warrants the amount the jury awarded.

Kinds of Damages

Civil cases don't result in jail time. The "punishment" or "remedy" is monetary compensation to the victim, or damages. There are a few different kinds of monetary damages. Compensatory damages are for direct compensation of the particular situation. Say you buy a painting for your antique shop for $10,000 that turns out to be fake. The seller refuses to refund you—you would certainly want back the money you spent. If your arm is injured in an accident that is not your fault, and your trip to the ER cost $20,000, you would want the cost of your medical treatment covered.

The courthouse is where legal justice can be sought.

But being compensated for the direct result of the tort is often not enough, because torts have further consequences. Let's go back to the painting example. If you displayed the fake painting in your antique shop as the real thing, and people found out it was fake and spread the word, it would hurt your business's reputation. Just getting the $10,000 you spent back would not be enough. You'd want to receive additional money to cover the harm the tort did to your business. Maybe you lost $10,000 in sales because your customers thought you were a cheater. Hiring a lawyer is another reason you'd want more than just the direct money lost due to tort, as part of your compensatory damages will have to go to pay your lawyer.

Looking at the injured arm example—if your arm was hurt so you couldn't use it and missed two months of work, you'd want to be paid for the time away. Maybe you're not able to perform your same job and you have to seek lower-paying work—the loss in wages over the rest of your working life could be calculated and priced. If it's a $10,000 a year difference, and you have thirty years until you reach retirement, that's

$300,000 in compensation, not even counting raises and inflation.

Damages might include the immediate and other consequences of your injury. If the ordeal with the fake painting led to gossip and negative reviews from which your shop never recovered, the financial damage to you might be severe. You might even have to close the shop and reopen it elsewhere with a new name. The cost of establishing a new business might be part of the damages you seek.

On top of all these concrete forms of compensation is compensation for "pain and suffering" or "mental anguish." Pain and suffering means physical pain that results from an injury—maybe a broken leg, a rash, or an infection—i.e., the initial pain due to injury and the resulting suffering of that pain. For example, your leg is broken, in pain, and you have to stay in bed for three weeks in a cast, suffering the consequences. Mental anguish is equally real—one tort can set off a string of bad fortune that causes you mental pain and makes you suffer. Maybe that mental suffering causes depression, or maybe it just makes you feel anxious for weeks or months. In any case, as anyone who has felt emotional pain over something will admit, that can make it hard to concentrate, do well in school or at work, and it can affect relationships. It is hard to put a price on mental anguish, but it's definitely a kind of suffering that is just as real as things that can be measured directly in dollars. Juries are often tasked to factor in pain and suffering when recommending an award of damages.

Punitive damages can also be awarded; they are not intended to compensate physical or mental pain but to punish the defendant for actions that are especially malicious, reckless, fraudulent, harmful, or even criminal in nature. Large companies may be able to afford paying compensatory damages for faulty products, but punitive damages, unlike compensatory damages, will take the wealth of the defendant into account. The bigger and wealthier the defendant, the more punitive damages might serve as a deterrent for them to commit future torts. Here's one real world example: in 2019 the manufacturer Johnson & Johnson was ordered to pay $37 million in compensatory damages to baby powder users who developed cancer as a result of asbestos present in the powder.

In 2020, a jury ordered the company to pay an additional $750 million in punitive damages, which shows how angry the jury was at they heard during the trial. (The judge later reduced the amount to $186.5 million due to a state law limiting punitive damages to five times the amount of compensatory damages.) Note that in a criminal case, the punishment may be a monetary fine, but this money goes to the state and not the victim of the crime.

How can companies afford to pay damages? First, they are often huge corporations with massive profits, and what they pay in damages is only a small fraction of their income. Second, they have insurance. Just as health insurance covers you in case you get sick, liability insurance covers companies, hospitals, schools, etc. in case they get sued. The price of liability insurance goes up if the number of claims goes up; the more insurance that is paid out, the more the insurance company charges to insure. Though liability insurance is not mandatory for all companies, those companies that want to do business with the government almost always have to have liability insurance (usually ranging from $1 million and up). This means they pay annual premiums to the insurance company, and if they get sued, their policy will cover a certain amount of the damages.

Nominal damages are awarded when the winning party receives a very small monetary award, often the symbolic amount of one dollar. This happens in cases where there is a strong sense that the defendant was wrong and did something wrong, but that the plaintiff is not able to prove that the harm requires compensation. The symbolic award of damages allows the case to stand in the record. In 2017, the singer Taylor Swift was sued by a radio DJ for $3 million on charges that she ruined his career by alleging he groped her in 2013. Swift filed a countersuit and a jury in Colorado ruled in Swift's favor, awarding her a symbolic $1 at her request because she wanted to send a message that "no means no."

Defendants want to pay as little as possible, if they pay anything, even when they know they are in the wrong. Sadly, it's human nature—why would anyone want to give out more of their money? Even with the most horrific disasters, it can be hard for justice to be served when defendants try to skimp on compensating victims. The tragic *General Slocum* steamboat fire in 1904 off the coast of New York City is one example. The chartered boat was filled with about 1,300 passengers on what was to be a picnic outing when a fire tore through the boat and it sank, killing most of those on board. The coroner's inquest found that the ship owners were negligent in many ways that contributed to the deaths of more than one thousand people, in everything from not having a properly trained crew to not having enough fire equipment. The owner of the Knickerbocker Steamboat Company was actually angry that people were suing him, and he filed a suit to limit the company's total liability to no more than the boat's value after it was burned—$5,000—which would mean only $5 per fatality. The owner also wanted to reduce that amount further by subtracting the salvage and wreckage fees. In the end, Knickerbocker wound up paying survivors and victims' families nothing. (Note: This same case in today's world might have had a very different result; as times change, so do the opinions of juries and judges about tort law cases.)

Small Claims Court

Most places around the country have an option called the Small Claims Court for those who want a faster, simplified way to file a civil lawsuit for less than $10,000 or so in damages (limits vary by location). This option involves only a judge and no jury, and the parties involved often represent themselves in court. They present their cases, offer evidence, and sometimes call witnesses, and then the judge makes a decision. These cases don't go on for days; most are presented within a couple of hours. The idea of the small claims court was made popular in the public eye by television shows such as *The People's Court* and *Judge Judy* that feature real-life cases. The parties in those cases both agree to have their disputes settled on the television show instead of an actual court of law. Small claims court cases are often heard in the evening to allow people who work the chance to not disrupt their day. Some small claims cases are tort cases, but many others are breach of contract cases, such as landlord-tenant disputes.

Exhibit of dangerous cars at the American Museum of Tort Law

CHAPTER SEVEN

LET'S SETTLE THIS

UP TO 95 PERCENT OF CIVIL LAWSUITS NEVER
even reach trial because they are settled out of
court before a trial happens. In many cases, it's
to both parties' advantage to settle, avoiding the
potential of the plaintiff getting nothing from
the defendant, or the opposite—the defendant
paying too much to the plaintiff. Legal fees can
add up to the hundreds of thousands and even
millions as a case drags on and on. Both sides
have to figure out their chances in court, and
the defendant has to calculate what the amount
of a potential settlement would be compared
to the price of fighting a long legal battle. How
solid is the evidence? How sympathetic are the

plaintiffs? How much suffering or monetary loss was there? Is it measurable?

This is an advantage of the tort system—sometimes, the threat of a lawsuit carries enough weight to bring large corporations to the table offering money. The other benefit of settling is to keep potentially damaging documents and witness depositions (embarrassing to one or both sides) between the two parties only. Once the case moves to the trial phase, any information presented is open to the public and media (as is the trial itself) and is part of the public record.

For corporations being sued, a settlement turns what might have been a long, drawn-out process into a quickly closed case. A settlement is not an admission of guilt—it's simply an agreement between the two parties to end the potential lawsuit before it goes to court or while it is already in court. A settlement can happen at any time before the case goes to the jury or even while the jury is deliberating. Of course, if a corporation is certain that it did nothing wrong and believes it important to take a stand, it may not want to settle a lawsuit.

Class Action

Class action lawsuits are uniquely powerful, because they rely on the power of sheer numbers of people and the power of the press and potential bad publicity. If one person has a problem with a product and sues, the case may never make the newspapers. If a product defect affects millions of people and a group of consumers decides to file a suit together on behalf of the entire group (or class) of people who may have been injured by the product, then the lawsuit could very well get press coverage, and the company being sued could feel pressure. A successful lawsuit filed by a single person could be costly enough, but a class action suit could have much more severe effects.

Often, a class action lawsuit (filed on behalf of several hundred or thousand people) will be settled such that a pool of money is distributed among the people who were wronged. Millions of dollars in settlement money can, after legal fees and divided by the number of people in the class, work out to a few dollars or less per person. In settlements, much of the money winds up going to the attorneys for the plaintiffs. Sometimes the settlement is not money but coupons or discounts. This can save the corporation money because only some people will use their coupons before the expiration date.

Here is an example of settlement language from 2010, when 1-800-Flowers was accused of unfairly adding a shipping charge on flowers delivered from local florists.

> *1-800-Flowers denies these claims, denies that it has done anything wrong, and denies that any Class Member was damaged in any way. The Court did not decide who was right. However, to avoid the expense of litigation, inconvenience, and interference with business operations, the parties have reached a settlement that they believe is in the best interests of the company and its customers.*

Settlements sometimes include "gag agreements" where both parties agree not to talk about the details of the case or its settlement—and this is often an incentive for the party being sued to settle the case, knowing the potentially damaging details will never go public.

Being part of a settlement class doesn't mean you have to accept the settlement. Once notified, you can choose to exclude yourself from the lawsuit or object to the settlement. You can fill out the claim form to get your portion of the settlement, or you can do nothing, in which case you are still part of the settlement class and become part of the settlement's provisions and concede the right to take any further action against the company.

Like a tort itself, a settlement does not have to be about something strictly related to consumer fraud—a settlement can arise from any kind of tort. One example was a suit against Facebook in 2012. The lawsuit said that Facebook illegally used names, profile pictures, photographs, likenesses, and identities of Facebook users to advertise products and services through something called "Sponsored Stories" without first obtaining the users' consent. For example, a Sponsored Story might show a user's name and picture, a user who was your Facebook friend, and say "Jimmy Jones plays Bouncy Castles." Since you like Jimmy, you might try playing Bouncy Castles. The game got free advertising through Facebook and used your friend as an unknowing pawn in their advertising.

Facebook agreed to pay $20 million into a fund that could be distributed to people whose identities were used in Sponsored Stories without permission. The settlement would provide up to $10 each to eligible members of the class . . . but if too many people applied for the money, then the $20 million would go instead to non-profit groups that teach people, especially children, how to safely use social media. How could that happen? Isn't $20 million a lot of money? It is—but look at the math. In theory, if two million people applied for the money, they'd get $10 each. If ten million people applied, they'd only get $2 each. If you include the cost of postage and mailing, that dollar value shrinks even more. If more than ten million people applied, that would cost more than $20 million—leaving $0 to enclose in the envelopes. So how did the settlement actually work out? In this case, those who applied started receiving checks for up to $15 each in 2016.

Contracts and Arbitration

A trial by jury is a right guaranteed by the Constitution, and Americans deserve to have that option. Settlement out of court is also an option that is used often, and it is the very threat (or promise) of a trial by jury, where the outcome is unpredictable and the legal fees can be high, that can bring companies to settle out of court. There is, however, another option in tort disputes called arbitration. The word is derived from the Latin *arbitrari*, meaning "to judge," but arbitration does not take place in a courtroom before a judge. Instead, a third-party private arbitrator is called in to settle the dispute and make a potential monetary award. The arbitrator is someone both sides agree to, who can be fair and neutral, listen to both arguments, review both sets of evidence, and make a decision. Unlike settling out of court, where the defendant is willing to offer money to the plaintiff, arbitration can wind up in either side's favor. In arbitration, you will not get nearly as much "discovery," or background information and evidence from the opposing side, as you would in a courtroom.

There are two types of arbitration—binding and non-binding. Binding arbitration is where both sides agree to follow the decision ahead of time, no matter what it might be. Both sides have a legal obligation to follow the arbitrator's ruling, and if they don't, it can be enforced by law. Non-binding arbitration, or mediation, is just a recommendation and can be accepted by both parties or rejected by one or both parties.

Arbitration is a method that both sides in a dispute sometimes agree to voluntarily. Other times, people agree to it without even realizing what they've done. Millions of consumers and workers don't realize they are signing (or clicking) away their right to a trial in favor of arbitration on a daily basis.

Arbitration language can be found within many contracts of all kinds. For example, take an AT&T wireless services contract in 2019, which stated "In the unlikely event that AT&T's customer service department is unable to resolve a complaint you may have to your satisfaction (or if AT&T has not been able to resolve a dispute it has with you after attempting to do so informally), we each agree to resolve those disputes through binding arbitration or small claims court instead of in courts of general jurisdiction."

So, what's wrong with that? Isn't arbitration fair?

Well, it is fair in a way, but it is far different from what happens in a jury trial, or even in a settlement. With arbitration, there is no negotiation with the defendant on the award. Arbitration is a situation where both sides' arguments will factor into the monetary award. The most notable aspect of arbitration is that it is *final*. There is no appeal. Once the arbitrator makes a decision, that's that. An arbitrator does not necessarily have to have special qualifications. Some arbitrators are former judges, others are attorneys, and others are just ordinary people.

To protect themselves from lawsuits, companies will sometimes put language in their contracts that you are agreeing to everything in the document when you sign on the dotted line. This "hold harmless" language might say that you waive the right to put the blame on them if something happens. This kind of language is more common than you might think.

Here is one version of a hold harmless clause in a contract:

> *XXX shall indemnify and hold harmless the Company, its officers, directors, employees, and agents from and against all actions, suits, proceedings, claims, demands, damages, losses, and expenses (including any attorneys' fees incurred and any amounts paid by the Company on the advice of its attorneys to compromise or settle any claim) caused by, resulting from, arising out of, or occurring in connection with any misrepresentation by XXX of, or breach by XXX of this Agreement or any of its provisions.*

Corporations offering online services will often place other limits in their Terms of Service, a document that you have to agree to by clicking a small box that says "I have read and agree to the Terms of Services below." Google prints some of their terms in all caps:

WE DON'T MAKE ANY
COMMITMENTS ABOUT THE

CONTENT WITHIN THE SERVICES, THE SPECIFIC FUNCTIONS OF THE SERVICES, OR THEIR RELIABILITY, AVAILABILITY, OR ABILITY TO MEET YOUR NEEDS. WE PROVIDE THE SERVICES "AS IS".

The vagueness of the language leaves it open for Google to defend their rights and for the courts to determine.

IS THIS A LEGITIMATE LAWSUIT? YOU DECIDE...

1) There's a spill of vegetable oil in a supermarket aisle that's been there for hours. It was not marked with any signs. Someone slips and falls, breaks a hip, and misses eight weeks of work.

   (ANSWER: *There may be a case here since the supermarket staff did nothing about the spill and had knowledge of it.*)

2) A shopper in a supermarket drops a container of vegetable oil, causing a leak. The shopper slips and falls, breaks a hip, and misses eight weeks of work.

   (ANSWER: *Since the shopper caused the problem, there is no way to blame the supermarket. And it is unlikely that the*

*shopper could blame the manufacturer of
the vegetable oil either, since many food
containers break when dropped.)*

3) A woman buys a 1940s antique car with
no seat belt. She is severely injured in an
accident. She wants to sue the manufacturer,
which is still in business, because the car
was unsafe.
(ANSWER: *Because automobile safety
standards have changed so much since the
1940s, it's not reasonable for the woman
to sue. It would be like someone suing the
maker of an eighty-year-old hand
iron because he got burned while using
the tool.)*

4) A man wants to sue a manufacturer, because his toddler got hold of a hunting knife they made and injured himself with it.
(Answer: It's a harder case to make if a child is injured by something that is not meant for children.)

5) A toy collector finds that a doll he bought for his collection has small ears that come off easily and could be swallowed by children. He decides to sue the manufacturer.
(ANSWER: Though the toy is dangerous, the man has not himself suffered any injury and so cannot sue for damages. He could however write a letter to the manufacturer warning them of the issue or survey parents to see if any of their children have been injured by the toy.)

6) A canned vegetable manufacturer issues a recall for a batch of corn due to potential pieces of glass in the cans. A customer buys the faulty corn at a store that knew about the recall but sold the cans anyway. He consumes the corn and is injured.
(ANSWER: The case here would be against the store owner for negligence, because the manufacturer did issue the recall.)

7) A man eats a fast food hamburger every day for ten years, develops heart disease, then sues the restaurant chain.
(Answer: Assuming the food chain makes its nutrition facts available to consumers, the man cannot sue for damages. Eating too much of anything could be damaging but that does not mean you could file a lawsuit.)

8) A woman develops a wound infection after surgery, which was one of the risks mentioned to her both pre-and post-operation. Her leg has to be amputated because she waited a month to get it seen and treated. She sues the hospital and the surgeon.
(ANSWER: Infection of surgical incisions is a commonly known risk. If the woman noticed the infection but did not do anything about it, it would be hard to make a case against the hospital or doctor.)

9) A man goes into the hospital to get his appendix removed. The surgeon mistakenly removes his spleen. The patient sues the surgeon.

(ANSWER: *There is a medical malpractice case here. The spleen cannot be reinserted and so the issue is not reparable.*)

CHAPTER EIGHT

WHO CAN YOU SUE?

You vs. Me

One person can sue another for damages, and many times, that is precisely what happens. You might think these cases involve smaller amounts of money because they are limited to the kinds of damage that one person can inflict. But imagine if Joey crashes his car into Jimmy's house and knocks down a wall. If someone is killed, that could result in a wrongful death lawsuit, where the value of a person's life (in the millions of dollars!) is the potential monetary compensation. (See the O.J. Simpson case discussed on page 28.) Of course, many person vs. person cases do involve smaller damages and wind up in small claims court. But they are still important to the people involved in the suit.

You vs. Corporations

As you've already learned, corporations may be big and powerful, but in the eyes of the law, they are as responsible for doing wrongs to others as individuals. Practically every size and type of company out there has been sued at one time or another. From two-person companies to giant corporations with thousands of employees, they are all liable for the safety of their products and their facilities. Statistics show that about 90 percent of all businesses are involved in a lawsuit at any given time!

You vs. the Government

Government entities can be as large and powerful as companies, so it is important that citizens can file lawsuits against local, state, and federal governments when they are wronged. Tort lawsuits against the government are nothing new. In the 1854–55 term of the US Supreme Court, the justices heard a case called *The City of Providence v. Daniel R. Clapp*. The case involved a man walking at night along a ridge of packed ice and snow on a city sidewalk who fell and broke his thigh. He filed suit against the City of Providence claiming that local law required the city to keep the highways free from snow obstruction. The jury found in favor of Clapp and awarded him $3,379.50 in damages.

On appeal to the Supreme Court, the City of Providence argued that there was no definitive rule about what kind of care should be taken by the city regarding fallen snow and also that "the towns and cities of Rhode Island are bound only to keep their highways and streets open, in case of falls of snow, so as to be passable for travellers, and not to keep them from being slippery from ice or trodden-down snow."

The plaintiff argued that the word "passable" means "safely and conveniently passable, as well when applied to side-walks, as to the other portions of the travelled highway." He also said that snow was an obstruction to pedestrians, and the safest thing to do was remove it entirely. Leaving snow to be stepped on and compacted, or left to freeze in ridges, was not acceptable because even a cautious person could slip and fall. The Supreme Court ruled in favor of the plaintiff, upholding the lower court's ruling— the city was responsible for sidewalks also, not just highways.

FROM US SUPREME COURT RULING ON
CLAPP V. PROVIDENCE

IN HIS OPINION FOR THE COURT, SUPREME
Court justice Nelson goes over the arguments
presented by both sides—the defendants
arguing that the City of Providence had done
enough to keep the sidewalk clear; and for the
plaintiff, claiming the City needed to do more.
After discussing both sides' arguments, the
Justice explained his decision to uphold the
lower court's ruling and find for the plaintiff that
the City should have kept the sidewalk clear of
snow and ice.

*The suit was brought in the court below against
the city of Providence to recover damages for
an injury occasioned by an obstruction on the
side-walk in one of its principal streets. The*

obstruction consisted of a ridge of hard-trodden snow and ice on the centre of the side-walk, along which the plaintiff was passing in the night time, and by means of which he fell across the ridge, breaking his thigh-bone in an oblique direction.

After the evidence closed, the counsel for the defendants prayed the court to charge the jury that the statutes of Rhode Island, requiring highways to be kept in repair, and amended from time to time, so that the same may be safe and convenient for travellers at all seasons of the year, as far as respected obstructions from falls of snow, merely required that the snow should be trodden down or removed, so that the highways should not be blocked up or incumbered with snow; but did not require that said highways should be free from snow or ice, so that the traveller should not be in danger of slipping thereon; and that the said snow being so trodden down and hardened into ice, and the side-walk not blocked up or incumbered therewith, but open and passable in the sense of the statute, in this case the defendants were not liable.

The counsel for the defendants, also, after referring to the statutes authorizing the city of Providence to build and repair side-walks, and also to the ordinances of the city passed in pursuance thereof, further prayed the court to charge, that neither the said statutes nor the ordinances defined or enlarged the duty or liability of the city as to the removal of snow from the side-walks, beyond that under the general statute of the State, nor were they evidence of the degree of care required of the city by the general statute; but that, notwithstanding the same, the city would not be liable under the general law, if the snow on the side-walk was trodden down so as to be open and passable.

The court refused so to charge; but charged, that, by the statute law of the State, the city was obliged to keep this street conveniently and safely passable at all seasons of the year; that, by a special act, the legislature having authorized the city to have side-walks designed for foot passengers, it was bound to keep those side-walks convenient and safe for pedestrians; that the law did not require absolute convenience or safety, but safety and convenience in a reasonable degree, having reference to the uses of the way and frequency of its uses; that, when a fall of snow takes place, so as to render a side-walk not conveniently and safely passable, it was the duty of the city to use ordinary care and diligence to restore it to a reasonably safe and convenient state. That the law does not prescribe how this shall be done, whether by treading down or removing the snow; and that it was for the jury to find, as matter of fact, whether the side-walk, at the time in question, was in a reasonably safe and convenient state, having reference to its uses; and if it was not so, whether its want of safety and convenience was owing to the want of ordinary care and diligence on the part of the city; and in considering whether due diligence required the city to remove the snow, the jury ought to take into consideration the ordinances, not as prescribing a rule binding on the city, but as evidence of the fact that a removal, and not a treading down of the snow, was reasonably necessary.

The 1st section of the statute of Rhode Island concerning highways and bridges, provides, 'that all highways, town-ways, and causeways, &c., lying and being within the bounds of any town, shall be kept in repair and amended, from time to time, so that the same may be safe and convenient for travellers, with their teams, &c.,' at all seasons of the year, at the proper charge and expense of such town, under the care and direction of the surveyor or surveyors of highways appointed by law. The surveyors are then authorized to remove all sorts of obstructions or things that shall in any way straiten, hinder, or incommode any highway or town-way, and when blocked up or incumbered with snow, they shall cause so much thereof to be removed or trod down as will render the road passable.

Among other provisions conferring upon the towns power to repair and amend the public highways, the 4th section enacts that each town, at some public meeting of the electors, shall vote and raise such sum of money, to be expended in labor and materials on the highways, as they may deem necessary for that purpose; and either the assessors or the town council, as the town may direct, shall assess the same on the ratable estate of the inhabitants, and all others owning ratable property therein, as other town taxes are by law assessed.

And the 13th section provides that if the town shall neglect to keep in good repair its highways and bridges, she shall be liable to indictment, and 'shall also be liable to all persons who may in anywise suffer injury to their persons or property by reason of any such neglect.'

It is admitted that the defendants are not liable for the injury complained of at common law, but that the plaintiff must bring the case within the above statute to sustain the action. It must also be admitted, that the act applies to cities as well as towns, and also to side-walks where they constitute a part of the public highway. This has been repeatedly held by the state courts in several States, under statutes substantially like the one under consideration.

The counsel for the defendants, conceding this view of the statute, and of the liability of the city generally, contends that, as it respects obstructions or impediments occasioned by the fall of snow, and accumulations of ice, the liability is qualified, and exists only in case of neglect to tread down or remove the snow, so that the track be not blocked up and incumbered thereby; and that, if the street or side-walk is passable by not being blocked up and incumbered with snow, as it respects this kind of obstruction, it is made safe and convenient within the meaning of the statute. And the latter clause of the 1st section of the act which directs that when the highways are blocked up or incumbered with snow, the surveyor shall cause so much thereof to be removed or trod down as will render the road passable; and also the 13th and 14th sections, which authorize the towns to impose penalties for the removal of snow from highways, and subjects the town to an indictment for neglect therein, are referred to as countenancing this modified liability.

But it will be found, on looking into the several decisions under a similar act in Massachusetts, that no distinction exists

between obstructions of a public highway
by falls of snow, and those of any other
description. In the case of Loker v. Brook-line,
Morton, J., speaking of the 1st section of the
statute, observes, that language so general and
explicit cannot be misunderstood or restrained.
It must extend to all kinds of defects, as well as
to all seasons of the year; and an obstruction
caused by snow is as clearly included as one
caused by flood, or tempest, or any other
source of injury.

The foundation of the action rests mainly
on the 1st and 13th sections of the statute.
The 1st imposes upon the town the duty of
keeping in repair and amending the highways
within its limits, so that the same may be safe
and convenient for travellers at all seasons
of the year; and the 13th declares, that if the
towns shall neglect to keep in good repair
its highways and bridges, it shall be liable
to indictment, and shall also 'be liable to all
persons who may in anywise suffer injury to
their persons or property by reason of any such
neglect.'

The other provisions, and among them
those referred to by the counsel, relate to the
powers conferred upon the towns to enable

them to fulfil the obligations enjoined, and to the powers and duties of the several officers having charge of the repairs of the highways. Ample means are furnished the several towns to discharge their obligations under the statute.

The act of 1821, amended by the act of 1841, confers powers upon the city of Providence, to build and keep in repair their side-walks, at the expense of the owners of the adjoining lots; and as may be seen from the several ordinances of the city, given in evidence, these powers have been liberally exercised for the purpose.

The powers of the towns and of the city are as ample for the purpose of removing obstructions from the highways, streets, and side-walks, arising from falls of snow and accumulations of ice, as those arising from any other cause; and the reason for the removal, so that they may by safe and convenient for travellers, is the same in the one case as in the others. The 13th section of the act which gives the personal remedy, makes no distinction in the two cases; and, in the absence of some plain distinction pointed out by the statute, it would be exceedingly difficult, if not impossible, to state one. It is conceded that an obstruction from falls of snow or accumulations of ice must be removed by the towns and cities, so as to make the highways and streets passable; and that this is a duty expressly enjoined upon them. The question is, what sort of removal will satisfy the requirement of the statute? It is admitted that, as it respects every other species of obstruction, the repairs must be such that the highways and streets may be safe and convenient for travellers; and that this is a question of fact to be determined by the jury. Is an obstruction by snow or ice to be determined by any other rule, or by any other tribunal? The counsel for the defendants suggests, that as it respects such safety and convenience of travellers in case of falls of snow, the statute should be construed as meaning merely that the snow should be trodden down or removed, as that the highways and streets should not be so blocked up or incumbered as not to be safely and conveniently open and passable. But it is quite clear that this would be a very indefinite and uncertain rule to guide either the officers, whose duty it is to remove these obstructions, or the jury in passing upon them when the subject of legal proceedings. The suggestion may be very well as an argument to the jury, for the purpose of satisfying them that the repairs in the manner mentioned were such as to fulfil the requirement of the statute, but to lay it down as a rule of law in the terms stated, might in many cases, and under the circumstances, fall far short of it.

The treading down of snow when it falls in great depth, or in case of drifts, so that the highway or street shall not be blocked up or incumbered, may in some sense, and for the time being, have the effect to remove the obstruction; but as it respects the side-walks and their uses, this remedy would be, at best, temporary; and, in case of rains or extreme changes of weather, would have the effect to increase rather than remove it. It is but common observation, and knowledge of those familiar with the climate of our northern latitudes, that not unfrequently the most serious obstructions arise from the great depth of snow and changes in the temperature of the weather; and that simply treading down the snow, and leaving it in that condition without further attention, would have the effect to render the highways and side-walks utterly impassable.

In the case also of obstructions from snow, the side-walks may frequently require its removal, so as to make a safe and convenient passage for the pedestrian, when, at the same time, the treading of it down in the street would answer the purpose for the traveller with his team. The nature and extent of the repairs must necessarily depend upon their location and uses; those thronged with travellers may require much greater attention than others less frequented.

The just rule of responsibility, and the one, we think, prescribed by the statute, whether the obstruction be by snow or by any other material, is the removal or abatement so as to render the highway, street, or side-walk, at all times safe and convenient, regard being had to its locality and uses.

We are satisfied the ruling of the court below was correct, and that the judgment should be affirmed.

New York City's government employs 325,000 people, more than the entire population of many large American cities! The decision of the New York Court of Appeals in *Bernadine v. New York City* (1945) exposed the city for the first time to liability for torts committed by its employees. In 2018, the City of New York paid $608.5 million in tort claim settlements. Of the 25,261 claims filed, 70 percent were for personal injury and 30 percent were for property damage. What kinds of torts might involve a city government? Motor vehicle accidents involving city vehicles (sanitation trucks, police cars, fire engines, ambulances, etc.), injuries occurring on school grounds, civil rights violations, medical malpractice in city-owned hospitals, injuries caused by defective sidewalks, and torts caused by city employees. Property damages can include flooding due to sewer and water main breaks and overflows, accidents with city-owned vehicles, poor roadway conditions (potholes, etc.) that cause damage to vehicles, missing stop signs or malfunctioning traffic lights, and lost or stolen items on school grounds.

There are plenty of instances where the government does not directly cause a tort, but because Congress or state legislatures or a federal agency fails to implement tougher safety standards or regulations, they make an injury more likely to occur.

One example of this is basketball star Kobe Bryant's 2020 helicopter crash in California. Some argue that if his chopper had been equipped with a terrain awareness and warning system (TAWS), it might not have crashed. This type of system was recommended by the National Transportation Safety Board, but the Federal Aviation Administration failed to make it mandatory equipment on helicopters. Bryant's widow later filed a wrongful death suit against the helicopter company, blaming the pilot's negligence.

You vs. the "Not Guilty"

When a defendant is found "not guilty" of a crime in criminal court (or maybe is not even prosecuted at all), this means they will not be going to prison for that crime. However, it does not mean they are off the hook. They can still be sued successfully in a civil lawsuit. The burden of proof in a criminal case is higher than that in a civil case. To be found guilty in a criminal trial, someone has to be proved guilty beyond a reasonable doubt, meaning the jury has to be very sure that the defendant did the crime. In a civil case, you just need to demonstrate a "preponderance of evidence" against the defendant to win.

The most famous example of this was the O.J. Simpson case, where the former football star/actor was arrested and tried for the 1994 murders of his ex-wife, Nicole Brown Simpson, and her friend, Ron Goldman. This case got massive media attention, and though Simpson was found not guilty in 1995 by the jury in criminal trial, he was later sued by the victims' families. An attorney in a civil case that follows an unsuccessful criminal case will try to use evidence from the criminal trial to his or her advantage, no matter if they are the plaintiff's attorney or the defendant's attorney. They will also try to tug on the heartstrings of the jurors to sway them.

And then, if the defendant is found guilty, the lawyers for the plaintiff will continue to try to influence the jury to settle on a higher amount of damages, while the defendant's attorneys will try to persuade the jury in the opposite direction. After Simpson was found guilty of the civil charges in 1997, the plaintiff's attorney told the jury in the closing statement that the punitive damages were going to set an example, as well as punish Simpson for "acts that were so willful, so malicious, so oppressive, and in such total disregard of human life." The defendant's attorney tried to convince the jury that Simpson simply did not have the money to give and that the plaintiff's attorney was trying to use passion to get them to award more money, when they should instead "follow the law." In the end, O.J. Simpson was ordered to pay a total of $33 million in damages to the victims' families. So, while Simpson was technically a free man, he was financially ensnared by the civil case decision.

Civil suits can be filed even when someone is indeed found guilty of a crime. Guilt does not prevent the injured parties from filing a civil suit. Remember: the crime is technically against the "state" whose punishment can often be prison time, while the tort is against the victim of the crime. While "justice" may be served by a prison sentence being handed down to a defendant, the wronged person does not get a tangible award from that verdict and may want to pursue a civil suit.

One famous example is the *Jackson v. AEG Live, LLC* case. Pop superstar Michael Jackson died in 2009 of an overdose of an anesthetic drug administered to him by Dr. Conrad Murray, his physician. In 2011, Dr. Murray was found guilty in a criminal court of involuntary manslaughter and sentenced to four years in prison. Jackson's parents then filed a $1.5 billion lawsuit against the concert promoting company in charge of Jackson's comeback tour, which the family claimed had hired Dr. Murray and was therefore negligent and responsible. But after all the evidence and testimony at the civil trial in 2013, the company, AEG, was found not liable for the death of the singer. The decision was appealed by the Jacksons but a California Court of Appeals affirmed the original verdict in 2015. Nonetheless, it was the Jackson family's right to seek damages. In a wild twist on the idea of wrongful death, thirty-four Michael Jackson fans in Europe sued Jackson's doctor in a French court for wrongful death, claiming "emotional damage" they suffered when the pop star died. The court decided five of the fans had proven their emotional damage and awarded them a symbolic one euro each.

Tort law is also a welcome remedy at times when a politically corrupt system, or a powerful and influential corporation or person, make it unappealing for a prosecutor to try a criminal case. That's the thing about the criminal law system—it is dependent on the police and government attorneys to pull together a case against someone. As a victim of a crime (especially a felony), it's usually not you who decides whether to bring charges against your assailant and make sure the case gets heard (domestic abuse cases can be the exception). You can tell your story, and the police and prosecutors collaborate and go from there. With tort law, it *is* up to you. You get to decide if and how you've been injured and whether you want to sue the person or company who is responsible. You are not dependent on the government to decide there is enough evidence to take your case before a judge and jury. Sometimes, successful civil lawsuits can lead to criminal prosecutions by helping to uncover witnesses and tell the whole story, as well as get media coverage and put pressure on authorities to prosecute and get criminal justice, in addition to civil compensation to the victims.

Civil Suits and Legal Fees

One big difference between criminal and civil cases is in how the victim is represented. In criminal cases, the case is brought by the state, so the victim's attorney is really the "people's attorney," prosecuting the case on behalf of the state to ensure that the criminal is punished for breaking the law. The prosecuting attorney in a criminal case is therefore paid for by the state. The victim does not have to pay a penny to have the case represented. Neither does the accused, as part of the well-known Miranda rights (which are the result of a famous Supreme Court case in 1966, *Miranda v. Arizona*) that are read to them states: "You have the right to an attorney, if you cannot afford one, one will be provided for you at no cost to you." In a civil case, however, it is entirely the plaintiff's responsibility to pay for an attorney to file and prosecute the tort case, and it is the defendant's responsibility to pay for an attorney as well.

The differences in salary are significant; the average salary for a prosecuting attorney in 2020 nationwide is about $72,000, much less than the salary for a medical malpractice attorney, which is well over $100,000 a year. State's attorneys are paid out via taxes, where tort plaintiff attorneys' salaries are paid from the settlements they win on behalf of their clients. Corporate attorneys, who are usually the ones defending their clients against lawsuits, are well-paid too. The better they are, the more money they save the corporation in costly settlements. And that does not just mean winning cases—it means being good enough to lose well. They must be convincing enough to the jury to downplay the corporation's liability and therefore cause the jury to reduce the amount of the award. To lose a case against a plaintiff seeking $25 million, but have the jury only award $2 million based on strong arguments from the defendant's counsel, while not the ideal outcome, would still be considered an improvement. Similarly, on the plaintiff's side, a victory and an award, even if a reduced amount, would still be seen as a positive. The stakes can be high in tort law cases, especially those against big corporations such as the Boeing 737 MAX tort litigation. The more money (and reputation) at stake, the more both sides will try to gather as many witnesses as possible and spend more time preparing their arguments. The longer cases drag on, the more they cost both sides. Bigger, complicated cases can cost millions in legal fees just to get to a jury verdict.

The good news is that many tort law attorneys will work on certain types of cases on a "contingency basis," which means the plaintiff pays nothing until the case is over, from the money recovered by the verdict or settlement. These are cases determined to have a high chance of winning, so if you win, the attorney gets a significant percentage of your award. If you lose, you still pay but only for expenses. Contingent fees also discourage frivolous lawsuits because attorneys won't take those cases unless they feel the case is strong and they can win. This type of fee arrangement levels the playing field and helps the average consumer take on huge automobile makers or tobacco companies that would otherwise be unaffordable to sue.

Torts Here, There, and Everywhere?
Practically any object can cause harm if used the wrong way. An average day in the life of a person can be filled with potential torts. You hurt your wrist trying to get paper towels out of the machine in a restaurant bathroom. The

mailman leaves your package in the rain, and the expensive contents get ruined. You get hit in the face with a soccer ball while playing. These are all "injuries," but they are not necessarily torts.

The elements of a tort case include the following important components:

1) *Duty*—What was the duty of the manufacturer or the provider of a service? A soccer ball maker's duty is to provide safe and usable soccer balls for use in the game of soccer. Duty of care can even mean simply following the rules, like paying attention while driving.

2) *Breach of duty*—The plaintiff has to prove that the wrongdoer did not meet their duty. If the soccer ball is faulty, that is a breach of duty on the part of the manufacturer. However, if someone is using a soccer ball as a seat and they fall off and hurt themselves, that is not a breach of duty because the ball was not meant to be used in that way.

Breach of duty can be unintentional, but it still can result in a lawsuit.

3) *Causation*—The plaintiff has to prove that the defendant caused the injuries. Just because there may have been a breach of duty does not mean that breach resulted in this particular injury. A soccer ball may have been faulty indeed, but if it caused an injury to Player A and not Player B, then Player B cannot file a lawsuit.

4) *Damages*—There are two senses of the word "damages." As discussed earlier, there must be some damage that occurred for a lawsuit to even happen. If a faulty soccer ball popped but nobody was hurt, then there was no damage done and there can also be no monetary compensation (damages) paid.

A soccer ball to the face can injure someone; does that mean that a lawsuit should be filed because soccer balls are dangerous? It's not so black and white. A ball is meant for playing sports and some games can cause injuries, just like watching games can cause injuries. The ball manufacturer is not at fault if you get hit in the face—their product is used in a game that can be dangerous. The soccer team is not at fault—joining the soccer team could be dangerous (and some team sports do require parents to sign an injury waiver). And the player who kicked the ball that hit you in the face is also not liable, because, again, it was not intentional—it was just part of a game that involves kicking balls. There are items far more dangerous than balls—saws, for example. If you were to cut yourself using a handsaw while cutting down a small tree, would you sue the saw maker? On the other hand, if you are using an electric saw with a faulty part that makes the blade slip and cut people, then the company could be liable. It's often down to this question: Did the item do what it was basically supposed to do, or not?

When could a ball cause an injury that is worthy of a lawsuit? Let's say there's a certain brand of soccer ball that has a defect causing it to suddenly burst when kicked too many times. Maybe it bursts in your face. That's an unexpected source of injury not related to the proper use of the ball; it's supposed to be kicked, just as a baseball is supposed to be hit many times with a bat. This is why some decorative things that look like toys—dolls, balls, or whatever—have warnings on them that say, "For decorative purposes only." If you were to hit a decorative baseball with a bat, it could shatter and injure you. If you were to give that decorative doll to a child, they could get injured because the doll was not made under the safety regulations required for children's toys.

Product warnings are necessary to protect both the consumer and the manufacturer. Look around your home or in the store at various toy boxes, food boxes, and other product containers. How many of them have warnings of some kind? You'll see many food packages containing phrases such as "this product contains wheat and dairy" or "this product was manufactured in a facility that processes peanuts." Because so many people have food allergies or sensitivities, these warnings are necessary—both to protect the consumer and to prevent lawsuits.

Tort law is not black and white. There are always shades of gray. The facts of each case are different, even if many things about the cases

There is a balance between the right to sue and abusing that right with fake lawsuits that exaggerate claims or seek damages for accidents that are nobody's fault. This cartoon from 1899 shows a judge holding a scroll with the "rules" of tort law trials. "Shyster" is a derogatory term for a lawyer who tries to cheat the system on behalf of a client.

THE INFRINGEMENT OF A RIGHT OR THE violation of a duty are necessary ingredients of a tort. If neither of these is present the act is not a tort, although damage may have resulted. Thus if a building be erected whereby a shop is hidden from view of the public, this, though causing great loss to the shopkeeper, is yet no tort; for no man has the right to an uninterrupted view of a particular spot if the land of another intervene. Therefore, though in this case there was damage, yet there was no infringement of a right or violation of a duty: in other words, no wrongful act.

The various acts which constitute torts may be classed as injuries to person, property, or reputation. But more particularly under the following heads: deceit, slander and libel, malicious prosecution, conspiracy, assault and battery, false imprisonment, enticement and seduction, trespass, conversion, infringement of

John Bouvier and Francis Rawle, *A Law Dictionary, Adapted to the Constitution and Laws of the United States of America, and of the Several States of the American Union* — Volume 2 (Philadelphia: J.B Lippincott & Co., 1883)

patents, copyrights, and trade-marks, damage by animals, violation of water rights and rights of support, nuisance, negligence, etc. In general, it may be said that whenever the law creates a right the violation of such right will be a tort, and wherever the law creates a duty, the breach of such duty couples with the consequent damage will be a tort also. This applies not only to the common law, but also to such rights and duties as may be created by statute. Thus a statute enacting that every ship shall carry medicines suitable to accidents and diseases at sea creates a duty; and any breach of this duty whereby damage results is a tort. That the statute in such tort provides a penalty for non-performance, to be recovered by a common informer, does not interfere with the private action. The penalty concerns the public wrong, and has nothing to do with the private injury or the private right of action.

CHAPTER EIGHT: WHO CAN YOU SUE?

are similar. It is for a jury to hear all the details and then decide whether the lawsuit makes valid claims and, if so, how much in monetary damages should be awarded. The judge then decides whether that amount is reasonable.

CHAPTER NINE

THE EVOLUTION
OF TORT LAW

TORT LAW IS MEANT TO BE A FAIR SYSTEM THAT
protects us from harm by others by providing
legal judgment and monetary compensation,
both as an award to those who have been injured
and as a deterrent to those who are wronging us.
But tort law is not unchanging. Over time and
with changing social values and new technology,
torts have evolved and so has tort law. With each
new type of case, new variations of "wrongs"
come up for courts to consider. With significant
case rulings, a new legal precedent is set. Let's
look at some important cases, both in the past
and in more recent times, and what they mean
for tort law plaintiffs and defendants.

You Can't Just Be Mean for No Reason

The idea of a straightforward tort has long been the basis for tort law. You damaged my property, so you have to pay for it. It's the more refined ideas about tort law that have evolved over time as the world around us has evolved.

Legal precedents have decided that torts can be committed for acts that might be seen as simply "mean" or purposely harmful, by harassing people just for the sake of it. This idea, which has deep roots in the justice system, is important for potential cyberbullying cases today.

An early case called *Keeble v. Hickeringill* took place in 1707 in England. The plaintiff, Keeble, had a pond on his property where he placed duck decoys and nets to attract and catch ducks he would sell at market. The defendant, Hickeringill, fired guns on a neighboring property to purposely scare the waterfowl away from Keeble's pond. Keeble sued, claiming that his livelihood depended on attracting the waterfowl and that he was being wronged. Hickeringill argued that Keeble did not own the ducks, so it should not matter if they were scared away. The ruling was in favor of Keeble because Hickeringill scared the ducks away knowing that Keeble was trying to attract them for use. He did it intentionally, and it did not matter that Keeble didn't own the ducks. The judge ruled that Keeble had a right to use his property to make money and attracting ducks was part of that right, so Hickeringill was liable for the loss of those profits. It was not actually the loss of the ducks for which the judge was awarding damages, but for the disturbance— the tort.

The ruling said, in part, "[W]here a violent or malicious act is done to a man's occupation profession or way of getting a livelihood, there an action lies in all cases." If someone hurts another person's profits by operating the same business, that is not a problem. If Hickeringill had set up decoys on his own property near Keeble's decoys there could be no lawsuit, because it would have been just as much Hickeringill's right to make decoys as it was Keeble's. For example, if Hickeringill was a schoolmaster who set up a new school right near Keeble's existing school and lured its students away, there would be no case. But if Hickeringill stood along the path to the old school with guns in hand, frightening the kids, then Keeble would have a case, and that was what happened with the decoys.

In *Walker v. Cronin*, an 1871 case in Massachusetts, a popular shoe manufacturer filed a suit against someone who intentionally caused forty-five of his employees to suddenly abandon their work, leaving the shoemaker scrambling to find other workers to finish the shoes. The defendant's attorney argued that the plaintiff could not sue over the defendant persuading shoemakers not to do their work, because he did nothing illegal in doing so. He claimed the workers had a perfect right to quit and that the defendant had a perfect right to convince them to do so. The judgment went to the plaintiff; the defendant appealed. In that court, the judgement was reversed, so the plaintiff appealed. The judge in the State Supreme Court didn't buy it. He ruled: "It is a well settled principle, that words, not actionable in themselves as defamatory, will nevertheless subject the party to an action for any special damages that may occur to another thereby." He continued: "Everyone has a right to enjoy the fruits and advantages of his own enterprise, industry, skill and credit. He has no right to be protected against competition; but he has a right to be free from malicious and wanton interference, disturbance or annoyance . . . " The shoemaker won the case.

Americans have become more intolerant of "meanness" or bullying in the last few decades. In addition to possible criminal prosecution, people who bully (whether in person or online) are also subject to tort lawsuits. Bullying can be verbal and/or physical abuse in person, or it can be over the internet—cyberbullying. A case called *Gannaway v. Grinnell-Newberg School District* (2015) involved not only taunting by students but a school principal who accused the victim of lying; that case was settled for an undisclosed amount. In 2018, an Alabama woman who claimed cyberbullying in a Facebook group was awarded $10,000 in damages for mental anguish and medical bills.

You Can't Lie to Consumers

Another important tort law concept is that corporations cannot lie to consumers or hide important facts. One early such case was *Langridge v. Levy* (1837), which dealt with fraudulent claims about merchandise. In 1833, an English man named George Langridge purchased a used double-barreled gun in a shop. The gun had a tag on it saying it was made by a famous gunmaker named Nock for a very famous client—none other than King George IV, who had died a few years earlier. The man was impressed, especially after the shop owner promised that the gun was a genuine Nock and was a good, safe gun. Langridge bought the gun and brought it home, where it was tested and worked fine. The man and his three sons used the gun every so often until one day a few months later his middle son was using the gun when one of the barrels exploded in his hand, causing so much damage that the hand had to be amputated.

In court, Langridge's attorney argued that the accident was due to the gun being unsafe and of poor quality, not at all the work of Nock. He said Langridge wouldn't have bought the gun had he known it wasn't a genuine Nock. Levy, the defendant, denied that he ever guaranteed the gun to be a Nock nor that it was perfectly safe to use. A jury awarded four hundred pounds to Langridge and Levy appealed the case. Levy's attorney argued that allowing this kind of responsibility for sellers was dangerous. He also took issue with the fact that Langridge's son was injured, not Langridge himself. Levy's attorney used an example to illustrate his point: "Supposing the owner of an unruly horse, knowing his disposition, sold him with a warranty that he was quiet to drive, and the buyer lent him to a friend, who put other persons into the carriage, and he ran away, and overturned and injured them; would the seller be liable to each of these persons?" The appeal was rejected and the ruling for the plaintiff, Langridge, was allowed to stand. A mere representation by the seller of the quality of the article sold does not furnish a ground of action against the seller on the representation turning out to be untrue, unless the representation be fraudulent. If the seller had just told Langridge, "This gun is several years old but it works, seems to be of good quality"—that would be different. However, because he represented it to be a high-quality gun made by a master gunmaker and once owned by a king, he made fraudulent claims.

One modern day example of this principle happened in 2017, when a California woman sued Coca-Cola for deceptive advertising practices that led her to believe drinking Diet Coke would lead to weight loss. A district court judge dismissed the suit, saying a "reasonable consumer" would not believe drinking Diet Coke alone would lead to weight loss. Another example of a tort case involving fraudulent behavior against consumers happened in 2019, when customers who purchased bed linens and towels made by the Welspun company filed a suit claiming that the products were deceptively labeled as "Pima Cotton" or "Egyptian Cotton"—two expensive types of cotton—when they were not. The company settled the lawsuit for $36 million.

Negligent Wrongs

What if, beyond simply lying to a consumer, you sell a product that you know can cause harm to its user? The key word is "know." Views on the harmfulness of various products have changed over the years. Cigarettes are a good example. Many decades ago, cigarette advertisements focused on how pleasurable smoking was and how good the cigarettes "tasted"—to the point where ads mentioned how many doctors preferred their brand over others. An old ad for Camels cigarettes claimed that 113,597 doctors smoked Camels. The one visible result of excessive smoking was coughing, so Lucky Strike took out an ad that proclaimed "20,679 physicians say Luckies are less irritating." An ad for Chesterfields had a headline that read "Scientific Evidence on Effects of Smoking" and offered a study concluding that people who smoked Chesterfields had "no adverse effects on the nose, throat and sinuses." It even featured a picture of Arthur Godfrey, a celebrity of the time, saying "Chesterfield is best for me!"

A government study in the early 1960s revealed shocking facts about how damaging cigarette smoke was, something cigarette companies knew already but had not shared with consumers. Starting in 1965, Congress required cigarette makers to place a health warning on their products. Starting in 1970, cigarette advertising on radio and television was banned.

Even today, it's estimated that 480,000 people a year die from smoking, and 41,000 people die from inhaling secondhand smoke.

The Cigarette Labeling and Advertising Act of 1965 required the following health warning, prescribed by Congress, to be placed on all cigarette packages sold in the United States: CAUTION: CIGARETTE SMOKING MAY BE HAZARDOUS TO YOUR HEALTH. The warning appeared on cigarette packs from 1966 to 1970. It was then modified to read this way from 1970 to 1985: WARNING: THE SURGEON GENERAL HAS DETERMINED THAT CIGARETTE SMOKING IS DANGEROUS TO YOUR HEALTH. The warnings were changed again in 1985, with four rotating Surgeon General's warnings required for cigarettes:

1) Smoking Causes Lung Cancer, Heart Disease, Emphysema, And May Complicate Pregnancy.
2) Quitting Smoking Now Greatly Reduces Serious Risks to Your Health.
3) Smoking By Pregnant Women May Result in Fetal Injury, Premature Birth, And Low Birth Weight.
4) Cigarette Smoke Contains Carbon Monoxide.

For decades, the tobacco industry hid data from the public showing cigarettes caused cancer and other diseases.

The McPherson v. Buick case was an early, important cause against the automobile industry.

Did the warnings mean that smokers could not sue? A landmark case was begun in 1983 by Rose Cipollone, a lifelong smoker of forty-two years from New Jersey who was dying of lung cancer. She brought a lawsuit against three makers of the cigarettes she smoked, and her family continued the suit after she died in 1984. In 1988, a district court ruled that two of the companies named could not be held liable because Cipollone started smoking those brands after warnings were added to the cigarette packs in 1966. But she had smoked Liggett Group's Chesterfield brand cigarettes since 1942, and they had not warned smokers of the health hazards of smoking even though they knew this information. The jury said she was 80 percent responsible for her cancer but still awarded her family $400,000, marking the first time that cigarette makers paid for health damage done by smoking. Liggett appealed the case, and in 1990, the Court of Appeals reversed the lower court's decision. Cipollone's family appealed, and the case went before the US Supreme Court. In a complicated 7–2 ruling, the Court said that the $400,000 award of the lower court was invalid, but the case could be refiled with more focused evidence proving that Liggett had conspired to withhold information about the dangers of cigarettes. The Cipollone family did not refile the case, but they had succeeded in disclosing important tobacco company documents to the general public.

Torts Evolve as Technology Does

With every new technological improvement, new kinds of tort lawsuits are born. The automobile was an invention of the late nineteenth century, and it did not take long before drivers were both suing and being sued. One case in Wales in 1901 saw Richard Powell sue Walter Mules for twenty pounds because Mules's car, traveling at fourteen miles per hour, plowed into Powell's horse and carriage. A famous case in the US called *McPherson v. Buick* (1916) involved a car that suddenly collapsed while the plaintiff was driving it, due to a wheel manufactured with defective wood from another company (not Buick). There was no evidence Buick knew about the defect, but it could have been discovered if Buick had inspected the car before selling it. The plaintiff's lawyer argued negligence on Buick's part. McPherson won the case and Buick appealed it. The appeal court, in a groundbreaking opinion by Judge Benjamin Cardozo (a future Supreme Court justice), upheld the lower court's decision, saying, "We think the defendant was not absolved from a duty of inspection because it bought the wheels from a reputable manufacturer. It was not merely a dealer in automobiles. It was a manufacturer of automobiles. It was responsible for the finished product."

Ralph Nader's investigation of General Motors (see chapter 1) was another important step in the fight against defective automobiles. General Motors faced more than one hundred lawsuits over the unsafe Corvair by the time Nader's book *Unsafe at Any Speed* was published.

In the 1970s, Ford faced about fifty lawsuits over its Pinto model, which was prone to bursting into flames due to a gas tank that easily exploded during a rear end impact, something documents revealed the company knew was a design flaw. The California case *Grimshaw v. Ford Motor Company* (1981) involved a woman who was killed and her passenger injured when her Pinto was rear ended by another car at thirty miles per hour, causing the gas tank to explode. A jury awarded the victims' families more than $3 million in damages and decided on $125 million in punitive damages to punish Ford for knowingly putting lives at risk with its car design. (The judge reduced the punitive damages to $3.5 million). That Ford engineers had options costing between one and eight dollars per vehicle that could have fixed the problem made the jury especially angry. In 1978, Ford recalled every last one of its 1971–76 Pintos (1.5 million cars) to make necessary fuel system adjustments. General Motors then issued a recall for 320,000 1976 and 1977 Chevettes for a similar reason. Nader had set into motion a powerful movement. Auto makers now knew they could be sued over their cars' safety, and between 1966 and 1972, twenty-five million vehicles were recalled by various automakers for safety reasons.

Years later, car makers are still being sued for defective vehicles. The National Transportation Safety Board received over two hundred complaints from drivers of 2013–2016 Ford F-150 pickup trucks saying that the brakes suddenly failed, leading to a class action lawsuit.

Lawsuits in the 1970s targeted the Ford Pinto, which had a tendency to burst into flames on rear impact

As technology continues to evolve and vehicles of all kinds become more complex, more varied, and more reliant on computers, there are more potential chances for things to go wrong. The faulty Boeing 737 MAX flight system mentioned in chapter 1 is one example. In 1986, the widow of the space shuttle *Challenger*'s pilot, who died along with his fellow crew members when the shuttle exploded after takeoff, sued NASA and the rocket maker, Morton Thiokol, for $1.5 billion in a wrongful death suit. Ultimately, the government and Morton Thiokol wound up paying a total of $7.7 million distributed among the victims' families.

Unintended Wrongs?

Wrongs don't have to be intentional. People (and companies) have certain liabilities for the products and services they sell. Tort lawsuits can involve negligence about almost anything, from the biggest items to the smallest. *Dickson v. Kincaid* (1808) in Scotland involved turnip seed. In 1802, Kincaid bought some turnip seed from a merchant, planted the seed and grew perfectly good turnip plants, from which he harvested more seeds and sold them to

Dickson, who in turn sold the seeds to others. One of these customers sued Dickson for damages when the seeds grew plants that were not normal turnip plants but some kind of strange and undesirable hybrid. Dickson was found liable and in turn he sued Kincaid, from whom he'd gotten the seeds, for damage to the good reputation of his seed business and to cover the damages that his customer was seeking against him. Upon investigation by a botanist, it was discovered that Kincaid had been growing other plants in the same plant family near the turnips, and those plants had cross pollinated with the turnips, resulting in the hybrid seeds. The court found that though Kincaid had acted in good faith and was no expert in botany, he was still liable for the problem.

Taking this idea further, say you give a friend a playful punch in the arm. He loses his balance, falls, and hits his head, getting a concussion. Does it matter that you didn't intend to injure your friend? You did cause his injury. If you hadn't punched him, he would not have fallen. This type of scenario really did happen in 1889 in a Wisconsin classroom, where one boy kicked another in the shin, causing severe damage by re-injuring an older injury. The kicker was found liable though he claimed "the touch was slight," because he had intended to kick the other boy. What if you were gesturing wildly and knocked him down by accident? Is that a lawsuit?

The idea of "negligence" varies depending on the circumstances. A Massachusetts case called *Brown v. Kendall* (1860) involved a man, Kendall, who swung a stick trying to separate two dogs from fighting. As Kendall, the defendant, raised the stick over his shoulder, it hit the plaintiff, Brown, in the eye, injuring him. The act was ruled unintentional, and the case went in favor of the defendant. On the other hand, in a Scottish case called *Byrne v. Boadle* (1863), a man walking along a road was hit by a barrel of flour that fell from the second floor of a shop. It was an accident, and the shop owner did not cause the barrel to fall, but the court found that the shop owner had a responsibility to ensure his merchandise was properly secured and would not fall to the street.

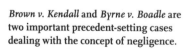
Brown v. Kendall and *Byrne v. Boadle* are two important precedent-setting cases dealing with the concept of negligence.

The Ambulance Chaser

Maybe you've heard the term "ambulance chaser" and wondered what it meant. It's actually a negative term referring to overeager attorneys who are literally following ambulances to the hospital from the scene of an accident, so they can turn the injured person into a new client who will sue over their injuries. It's a term used to try to spin tort attorneys and lawsuits in a bad light. You have probably seen television commercials with a man staring out at the audience, asking very gravely: "Have you been injured?"

This is not a new phenomenon. Attorneys have been looking to attract "wronged" clients for a long time. Most times, this is perfectly fine; it helps people who otherwise might not be motivated to seek compensation for their injuries. Commercials can also raise awareness of the kinds of injuries for which people could seek compensation. There are, of course, occasions when the "ambulance chasing" can be a little severe—which brings to mind a story about the author's great-great uncle, William Bach, who had a plumbing shop in New York City. One day in 1905, Bach was overseeing a crew working in a sewer manhole when an iron bar struck a stone, causing a spark that led to a gas explosion.

The men were working in front of an automotive garage, and gas from that business had seeped into the ground and triggered the explosion. Bach was horribly burned on his arms and body and taken unconscious to the hospital by the horse and wagon of his father-in-law. Later, when he was feeling a little better, Bach hired an attorney named Dalberg to sue the automotive garage for their carelessness in letting gas leak into the sewers.

But when Bach arrived in court, he was in for a surprise. The defendant complained to the judge that he was being sued twice for the same thing by the same person! Bach was confused, but it was true—another attorney had already started a suit against the garage on behalf of Bach. This attorney explained that soon after Bach had arrived in the hospital, he'd visited Bach and got permission to file a lawsuit. Bach remembered nothing of the sort and insisted that neither he nor his wife had authorized this lawyer to file a suit. The judge listened carefully to this story but decided to make Bach pay $10 (about \$288 in today's money) to the garage for their defense costs on the first, unauthorized case. If the first attorney had visited Bach, he was probably half-conscious and in great pain—in no condition to make decisions or remember what happened later on. The overeager "ambulance chaser" had cost money to the injured man who was seeking money for his injuries.

CHAPTER TEN

COFFEE, CAKE, AND TOYS, OH MY!

The Hot Coffee Case

One of the most famous tort law cases of the twentieth century is the "hot coffee case," a.k.a. *Liebeck v. McDonald's Restaurants* (1994). The case involved a seventy-nine-year-old woman who sued McDonald's when she was burned by their hot coffee. She was awarded $3 million in damages by a jury. The lawsuit seemed silly to many who casually heard about it at the time (the author remembers thinking that exact thought back then!), and became a "perfect" example for people who believed that civil lawsuits in this country had gone too far—too much money being given out for too many trivial lawsuits. However, the facts show this was not some careless old lady trying to get rich from an accidental spill. She didn't just say "ouch" and file a suit. No, Mrs. Liebeck was in the hospital for eight days and required skin grafts to heal her deep burns.

In the McDonald's case, the temperature of the coffee was the key issue. The recommended hot beverage temperature for McDonald's stores at the time was 180–190 degrees. (For reference, boiling temperature is 212 degrees; the average temperature of coffee people make themselves at home is 135–140 degrees.) The 180-190 degree range is hot enough to cause third-degree burns in just seconds, and that is what happened to Mrs. Liebeck.

Mrs. Liebeck originally wanted $20,000 to cover the expenses for treating her injuries, but McDonald's highest offer was only $800, and that is why she decided to file suit. Though she was awarded $200,000 for pain and suffering and $2.7 million in punitive damages (because of the number of previous coffee temperature complaints McDonald's had received without changing their temperature policy), the judge reduced the pain and suffering award to $160,000 because he found her to be 20

The McDonald's "hot coffee" case is one of the better-known tort law cases, but wrongly received a reputation as a frivolous lawsuit.

percent responsible and reduced the punitive damages to $480,000. Liebeck and McDonald's later settled the case for an undisclosed amount because both sides knew appeals would prevent the case from being resolved for a long time. Still, it was an important victory and not at all the frivolous lawsuit that the media made it out to be.

There is no guidebook that says how hot coffee should be or how dry a floor should be. It's up to a jury to decide these things, and once they do, that case can become a legal precedent that future attorneys can use in their arguments. Because the McDonald's case jury awarded $3 million for coffee that was 180–190 degrees, another case with hotter coffee would make a good argument to a jury. However, if the temperature was 130 degrees, there would be a much smaller chance of success.

The Tort about a Tort

As times change, the kinds of torts we see change, too. Tort law is definitely not a piece of cake, even when it's about a cake. In 2012, a gay couple looking for a wedding cake visited the Masterpiece Cakeshop in Lakewood,

Colorado. Shop owner Jack Phillips refused to bake the wedding cake, but was willing to sell them other kinds of cakes. "I'll make your birthday cakes, shower cakes, sell you cookies and brownies. I just don't make cakes for same sex weddings," he told them. He later said that his refusal was based on religious opposition to gay marriage. At the time, Colorado did not yet recognize the legality of gay marriage; the couple was planning to marry in Massachusetts and later have a reception for family and friends in Colorado.

The couple believed that the baker's refusal violated the Colorado Anti-Discrimination Act, which said: "It is a discriminatory practice and unlawful for a person, directly or indirectly, to refuse, withhold from, or deny to an individual or a group, because of disability, race, creed, color, sex, sexual orientation, marital status, national origin, or ancestry, the full and equal enjoyment of the goods, services, facilities, privileges, advantages, or accommodations of a place of public accommodation." After the baker refused them, the gay couple filed a complaint with the Colorado Civil Rights Commission, which referred the case for a formal hearing before a state administrative law judge, who ruled in the couple's favor.

The bakery owner claimed that being forced to create a cake for such an event would violate his right to free speech, requiring him to use his talents for something he disagreed with personally. However, the judge disagreed with that as well as the claim that the baker's free exercise of religion was violated. After the ruling, the Commission affirmed the decision, and so did the Colorado Court of Appeals. The case, *Masterpiece Cakeshop, Ltd. v. Colorado Civil Rights Commission* went to the US Supreme Court in 2017, which ruled in 2018 that the Commission was showing anti-religious bias. According to the decision: "Our society has come to the recognition that gay persons and gay couples cannot be treated as social outcasts or as inferior in dignity and worth. For that reason the laws and the Constitution can, and in some instances must, protect them in the exercise of their civil rights. The exercise of their freedom on terms equal to others must be given great weight and respect by the courts. At the same time, the religious and philosophical objections to gay marriage are protected views and, in some instances protected forms of expression."

This case was a difficult one because it involved the clash of two fundamental American rights: protecting every citizen from discrimination versus the rights of free speech and free exercise of religion. The Court overturned the lower court's ruling and ruled in favor of the baker, 6–2. Though the couple were reasonable in believing they had the right not to be discriminated against in public, that did not extend to a universal right to have a cake baked for them. It ran up against the baker's constitutional right to reject creating something for customers that contained a message he would not approve of based on his religious beliefs.

In Justice Ginsburg's dissenting opinion, she pointed out that the couple just wanted a wedding cake, not one with a message or symbol on it—a wedding cake like any other the baker would sell. The refusal was based on the identity of the customers, not any message on the cake itself.

Did the Supreme Court rule correctly, or was the couple's protection from discrimination violated by the baker's refusal to make them a cake? What if a Christian baker refused to make a plain chocolate cake for a Jewish couple during Hanukah? Would that be the same thing?

Torts and Kids

Not all torts involve adults. There are plenty of torts involving kids. Sadly, some medical malpractice cases involve children who are seriously injured through the fault of doctors, surgeons, or hospitals. There are also plenty of cases involving injuries due to dangerous toys. We've all seen age warnings on toy packages, often consisting of a picture of a circle with a bar through it and "ages 3 and up" or something similar written on it.

Toys were not common until relatively recently. In colonial times, there were some toys and games, and of course dolls, but most people could not afford to buy toys for their children. Average children did not have much time for playing anyway, as they were too busy with chores, homework—or with jobs they got at very young ages. If anything, children (or their parents) made their own toys out of materials that were available.

By the late nineteenth century and early twentieth century, store-bought toys were gaining in popularity and affordability. With the advent of comic books, radio shows, television, and movies, and cheaper prices, toys were common in almost every household. But safety was not a major factor in toy design until recently. For most of the twentieth century, toys were made without regard for potential dangers posed to children. Even now, new toy issues arise every year and toys get recalled because they are unsafe.

One of the most common issues are choking hazards. Little children love to put things in their mouths, and the toys of old used to be small enough that they could get stuck in babies' and toddlers' mouths and throats.

One important case was *Cunningham v. Quaker Oats, Fisher Price Division* (1986). This case was about a fourteen-month-old child who choked on a little Fisher Price toy figure in 1971, causing brain damage. Fisher Price had known of the dangers of these little toys six years earlier but did not do anything about it. The child's parents sued in 1973, and the lawsuit dragged on for years until it ended in a

original figurines have not
remain in homes and
try.

FISHER · PRICE TOYS

AaBb Cc

192

A popular school bus toy found to be unsafe for use by small children, on display in the American Museum of Tort Law.

$2.25 million settlement from the toy company. (At the time, it was the largest such settlement ever.) The original figurines were never recalled (the author played with them as a child too!), but Fisher Price changed the labeling on the toys and made them larger to reduce the choking risk.

Those two things are the keys to modern toy safety—larger size and proper age-related warning labels. These days, toys made for the very young are purposely made big enough that they cannot be choking hazards.

Another common danger is sharp edges. Toys used to be hard and sharp. Wooden letter blocks used to be solid wood. Toy cars used to have thin metal parts. And toys like dart sets used to be common—the darts weren't razor sharp but still sharp enough to puncture a child's skull. Pull toys with ropes or cords are choking hazards.

Even the decoration on toys can be dangerous. In 1977, 8,400 sets of wooden alphabet blocks were recalled by the manufacturer because they contained dangerous levels of lead paint.

In 2008, the Consumer Product Safety Improvement Act of 2008 (CPSIA) mandated that the voluntary toy safety standard in effect at that time become a nationwide mandatory children's product safety rule. There are forty-one different types and aspects of toys that require safety testing, everything from toy wheels and tires to stuffing materials, from toys with nails or wires to toys that produce sound or contain magnets.

With toy torts, as with all torts, there has to be a balance of reasonable expectations and responsibility. If a toy is labeled "Ages 10 and up" and it winds up in a preschool being used by a two-year-old, who gets injured, that is not the manufacturer's fault, but it could be the preschool's fault. If the same toy is not labeled at all or is labeled as safe for toddlers, then it could be the manufacturer's fault. There could be gray areas with product ages too. If a toy is labeled for ages three and up, and a child is injured by it the day after their third birthday, does that mean the manufacturer should be sued? The judgment of the parent or teacher is important too. Some small children are bigger and develop faster than others. It would be unwise for the parents of a smaller and/or slower-developing child to give them a pile of "Ages 3 and up" toys on their third birthday, just like parents of an advanced two-and-a-half-year-old might be okay giving that child more advanced toys.

It's especially important for kids to be protected from danger. For one thing, kids are less able to protect themselves from injury, and second, kids cannot take legal action without adult assistance. When adults are involved in torts, they can speak for themselves. Smaller children may not be able to give depositions. In those cases, the parents or guardians and doctors who treat the kids have to advocate for the children. Kids of school age, who can talk and string together sentences, are usually deposed, questioned by attorneys for both sides. Attorneys for both sides try to make sure that what the adults say happened really did happen. Attorneys for the defendants have to look out for children who have been coached on what to say or who are obviously lying at the direction of their parents. Attorneys for the plaintiffs have to make sure the children's stories are heard and believed.

As mentioned, toys do get recalled, but this is not an ideal solution. When a car manufacturer recalls an automobile, chances are they would have your name and address and be able to contact you. The problem with recalls for smaller items is that there is no way to track everyone who has purchased them. In many cases, unless you are looking on a recall web site (such as www.safekids.org or www.cpscgov) or the recall happens to be mentioned on the news, you may never know. The answer really lies in better product development and testing, to incorporate safety first instead of after the fact.

Environmental Torts

It's bad enough we have to face daily dangers in the products we buy and use. Even worse is the fact that often the very food we eat, water we drink, and air we breathe is polluted by either intentional or reckless behavior by large corporations. When people get sick or die as a result of what these companies knowingly did to the environment, they must be held accountable.

One of the most notorious events of environmental pollution occurred in an upstate New York community known as Love Canal. The story began in 1942, when the Hooker Chemical Company began dumping toxic waste into an abandoned canal in Niagara Falls. A large housing project was built over the dump without residents knowing of the area's toxic history. Several decades of this toxic dumping led to serious health issues for people in the area, and an expensive government cleanup. In 1995, the Occidental Chemical Company agreed to pay $129 million to the federal government to cover the costs of the massive cleanup. Legal action was still going strong as of 2020, when a class action lawsuit was filed on behalf of residents who had suffered health issues due to continued contamination problems in the area.

Often, chemicals that are first deemed safe turn out to be harmful, and lawsuits can arise if companies knew about this new information but did not warn consumers. Bisphenol A (BPA) has been used since the 1960s in plastics. During the 2010s, some states began to ban the use of BPA for use in products intended for babies. A study done by the Centers for Disease Control and Prevention (CDC) found BPA was present in 93 percent of urine samples from Americans over the age of six. Exposure to BPA has been associated with various medical conditions and issues, including heart disease. Several lawsuits have been filed in recent years against manufacturers of products containing BPA, including cans, baby bottles, and baby formula.

Asbestos is another substance that was commonly used for years but was found to be harmful. Between 1940 and 1979, twenty-seven million workers in the US were exposed to toxic asbestos fibers. In 1969, one of those workers filed a suit against the manufacturer, claiming they knew the substance was harmful. His family won the case, but he died before the verdict was issued.

Charged with Overcharging

Have you ever really wanted to go see your favorite YouTube star in concert? Maybe you begged your parents to go online and buy tickets. The tickets only cost thirty-nine dollars and you really want to go with a friend. But when your parents buy the tickets, they pay the ticket price plus fees, adding up to more than sixty dollars per ticket! But they had no choice—there was only one place to buy the tickets.

While it's legal for companies to charge fees of all kinds for products and services, they must do it honestly and transparently, meaning they must explain clearly what people are paying for. When they don't, lawsuits can arise. Excessive ticket fees were the subject of a class action lawsuit called *Schlesinger v. Ticketmaster*. The suit was filed on behalf of a nationwide class of consumers who purchased tickets on Ticketmaster's website between 1999 and 2013. In addition to the ticket cost, consumers paid an additional "Order Processing Fee," and a subgroup of consumers also paid extra for speedy delivery of their tickets via United Parcel Service (UPS). The suit claimed that Ticketmaster's fees were "excessive and deceptive."

For each transaction, settlement class members received a code for a $2.25 discount, and they could apply two additional credits per ticket purchase—UPS discount codes worth five dollars and ticket codes redeemable for potentially free concert tickets. This is an example of a settlement where both sides probably thought they came out well. The ticket buyers were pleased to get their fees back in the form of discounts and free tickets. Ticketmaster only had to pay for the codes that were redeemed in the four-year period the settlement required.

Tort Reform, a.k.a. Tort Deform

The mid-1960s to mid-1970s were a time of growing consumer protection and awareness. Increased government regulation of everything from products to air and water pollution seemed to protect Americans from exposure to many types of dangers. But since then, things have changed. Deregulation, or the reduction of government control, started with the Ronald Reagan presidency in 1981, and continued over the years since. As a result, corporations have become more powerful again. According to Ralph Nader, who helped lead the consumer protection movement, corporations "have taken over much of the Democratic Party that we relied on in the 1960s, weakened the labor unions— with globalization, automation, restrictive laws like the Taft-Hartley Act . . . Also, corporations have conglomeratized and commercialized the media as never before."

As corporations have grown more powerful once again, they have led an attack on tort law, under the tricky name of "tort reform." In the context of politics and society in general, the word "reform" sounds like a good word, a positive one that brings change for the better.

Asbestos was used in manufacturing for decades, sickening many workers who inhaled the toxic fibers.

The word literally means "to make again"—it's like a fresh start. Reform the criminal justice system! Reform school was a place where juvenile offenders were sent to change their lives. Someone who's been reformed has changed themselves for the better. So you might think that "tort reform" would be a positive thing for us all. But the word "reform" is sometimes a tricky one, because it depends on who is using it and for what purpose. Those who have been trying to push a tort reform agenda are not average citizens trying to get more rights against big corporations—they are none other than the very corporations (and the political candidates who are funded by them) who are potentially held accountable for their wrongdoing by lawsuits. Their idea of tort reform makes the term "tort *de*form" more accurate. Tort reformers want to pass legislation that makes it harder for the average person to file a lawsuit and limits their rights once in court. They also want to limit the possible damages on medical malpractice cases.

During the 1970s and 1980s, tort law was assaulted by insurance companies and politicians. Some argue that tort law cases make insurance rates go up because of the high punitive award amounts given to successful plaintiffs. But it's really the opposite—a successful legal case about a defective product brings the issue to light, which forces the company in question to make their product safer.

There was a notorious case that was much talked about in the '80s involving a man who picked up his lawn mower to use it like a hedge clipper and injured himself. He then won a $500,000 judgment in a lawsuit. But it was fake; it never happened. In a 1986 speech, President Ronald Reagan referenced a tort law case where a man in a phone booth was badly injured when a drunk driver crashed into it. "Now it's no surprise that the injured man sued," Reagan said. "But you might be startled to hear whom he sued: the telephone company and associated firms." Reagan implied that the suit was an example of an out-of-control legal system. In reality, the phone booth door had been malfunctioning and trapped him inside so he could not escape in time to avoid the collision. And he did also receive some money from the drunk driver.

FROM THE US SUPREME COURT DECISION ON *BMW OF NORTH AMERICA, INC. V. GORE* (1996)

IN THIS OPINION BY JUSTICE JOHN PAUL Stevens speaking for the majority, he explains that the jury's punitive damages award in the case was excessive in comparison to the compensatory damages awarded, and that such high punitive damages were not allowable in a case where the defendant's conduct was only "minimally reprehensible."

This case comes to us on a writ of certiorari to the Supreme Court of Alabama.

In 1990, the respondent Dr. Gore purchased a new BMW sports sedan from an authorized BMW dealership.

Nine months later, although he had not noticed any flaws in the appearance of the car, Dr. Gore was informed that parts of the

car's exterior had been repainted, apparently because the car had suffered acid rain damage after it left the factory in Germany.

Dr. Gore filed suit against petitioner BMW of North America seeking compensatory and punitive damages for BMW's failure to advise him that the car had been partially repainted.

Compensatory damages are intended to compensate the victim of a wrong; punitive damages are meant to punish past wrongful conduct and deter its repetition.

At trial, BMW acknowledged that it had a nationwide policy under which the damaged car was sold as new without disclosure of repairs if the repairs cost less than 3 percent of the car's suggested retail price.

At the time the policy was adopted in 1983, through the date of Dr. Gore's purchase, BMW's policy was at least as stringent as any State's statutory disclosure requirement.

Thus, for example, eleven State legislatures require disclosure of only pre-sale repairs costing more than 6 percent of the suggested retail price.

Because refinishing Dr. Gore's car cost less than BMW's 3 percent threshold, the repairs were not disclosed.

In support of his claim for punitive damages, Dr. Gore introduced at trial evidence that BMW had sold as new without disclosure approximately one thousand repaired cars nationwide.

Fourteen of those sales occurred in Alabama.

The jury awarded Dr. Gore $4,000 in compensatory damages and $4 million in punitive damages.

On appeal, the Alabama Supreme Court found that the jury had improperly computed the amount of punitive damages by multiplying Dr. Gore's compensatory damages by the amount of similar sales in the entire United States.

The court therefore held that BMW was entitled to a reduction and jury award and the $2 million was inappropriate punitive sanction under the circumstances.

In previous cases we have held that the Due Process Clause of the Fourteenth Amendment prohibits the imposition of a "grossly excessive" award of punitive damages.

We granted certiorari in this case to consider BMW's claim that the $2 million sanction imposed in this case is so excessive as to violate its constitutional right to due process.

In an opinion filed with the Clerk today, we reverse the judgment of the Alabama Supreme Court.

We agree with that court that reliance on BMW sales in other States was improper.

No State may punish a defendant for out-of-state conduct that did not affect the State's residence and that was presumptively lawful where it occurred.

To do so would interfere with the policy choices of other States.

We therefore consider the constitutionality of this award in light of the conduct which Alabama may legitimately seek to punish and to deter.

That is the sale of repainted cars in Alabama without disclosure.

Elementary notions of fairness dictate that a person receives notice not only of the conduct that will subject him to punishment but also the severity of the penalty that may be imposed.

Three guideposts, each of which indicates that BMW did not receive adequate notice of the magnitude of the sanction Alabama might impose, lead us to conclude that the $2 million punitive award for selling this repainted car is grossly excessive.

First, the conduct was only minimally reprehensible.

The harm inflicted was purely economic, no one's health or safety was put at risk, and there is no evidence that BMW is a repeat offender.

Second, the 500:1 ratio of punitive damages to compensatory damages is unusually large in the absence of particularly egregious conduct.

Third, the punitive award is substantially greater than the statutory fines available in Alabama and elsewhere for comparable misconduct.

Most legislative bills are born from one interest group or another pushing them, and the insurance industry has been a major force in helping advance laws that would clamp down on the rights of plaintiffs—all 50 states have enacted some kind of measure to limit patients' compensation in medical malpractice cases.

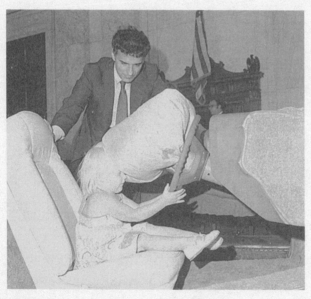

Ralph Nader demonstrating automobile air bags

In a 1991 speech to the American Bar Association, Vice President Dan Quayle said, "Let's ask ourselves: Does America really need seventy percent of the world's lawyers? Is it healthy for our economy to have eighteen million new lawsuits coursing through the system annually?" Studies show that the actual amount paid out in civil (medical malpractice and product defect) lawsuits is just a tiny fraction of the money these companies make and the money insurance companies get in premiums from customers.

One attempted assault on tort law happened in 1988. A set of ballot propositions in a California election would have severely limited the contingency fee to which lawyers and clients agree. This would have demolished the contingency fee system, and those people who were unable to pay for legal fees up front would no longer be able to sue. Citizen groups defeated these propositions in the election and won Proposition 103 that reformed regulation of auto insurers (which the industry spent a whopping $80 million to try to defeat). Other states, however, have implemented contingency fee restrictions at the urging of the insurance industry.

Despite the fact that we actually are not a very litigious society (meaning we do not file a lot of lawsuits), bit by bit, tort law deformation has taken place around the country at a steady pace since the 1980s. Several states have enacted limits on awards for punitive damages. In 1996, the US Supreme Court found that a punitive damages award of $2 million in the case of *BMW of North America, Inc. v. Gore* violated the Fourteenth Amendment, or due process rights. That suit was over an automobile that had been repainted before purchase, unbeknownst to the buyer, Dr. Ira Gore. The Court ruled that punitive damages cannot be "grossly excessive," which it believed they were in this case.

CHAPTER ELEVEN

PEOPLE POWER——EVERY VOICE COUNTS

Tort Law Is a Deterrent!

One of the best ways to fight corporate power is to sue if you are wrongfully injured by the actions (or inactions) of a large company. Because the tort law system exists in America, it protects millions of people just by being there— just like the criminal law system can help deter people from committing crimes. The truth is Americans are less likely to be injured when everyone knows that negligence and carelessness can lead to costly lawsuits. Civil lawsuits bring light to dark places and expose secrecy, revealing wrongdoing that can put people like you at risk. Once dangers are exposed for all to see,

Ralph Nader (and Edward Markey, also a speaker) addressing several hundred members of Massachusetts Fair Share, at a rally in Boston Commons, ca. 1980.

companies are under pressure to make their products safer.

Sometimes all it takes is one incident and one lawsuit to get the attention of a manufacturer and prevent additional people from being hurt. Let's say there's a toy with an easily breakable part that injures a child named Timmy. The lawsuit that follows would probably result in money paid to Timmy's family, but it would also motivate the toymaker to correct the problem before anyone got hurt and sued. Another problem for corporations is that they can't predict what will happen in a second lawsuit based on what happened in the first lawsuit. If a jury awards someone $50,000 for an injury due to a faulty washing machine, there is no guarantee that the next jury for the next case wouldn't award $100,000 or $1,000,000. It depends on the makeup of the jury, on the details of the particular case (for example, how severe was the injury?), the ability of the plaintiff's lawyer to convince the jury, and how sympathetic the plaintiff is in the courtroom.

Previous legal cases are also used by attorneys as examples in their legal arguments. If another child, Vicky, gets hurt by the same toy as Timmy, Vicky's attorney will surely cite Timmy's case. And if a company is repeatedly found liable for an injury of the same type due to the same product defect they never bothered to fix, you can imagine that the damages amount might go higher and higher. The plaintiff may feel emboldened to ask for more money, and the jury may feel it is right to award it to punish the company's continued ignorance of the problem. It is a more serious offense when a defendant has continued a behavior that maybe the first time around was just ignorance or carelessness—once a person or corporation is aware of a problem then it becomes more of an intentional tort as opposed to carelessness. Testimony taken from witnesses in tort law cases can be useful in future cases.

But the tort law system is not just good for plaintiffs. It can benefit innocent defendants, too. For example, if Timmy lost the case because the jury decided he was using the toy in a way that was not intended, then this could help protect the toymaker against similar future lawsuits. Legal precedents can help both sides make their cases.

The tort law system can also prevent frivolous lawsuits from being filed. All it takes is one or two similar cases that were dismissed by a judge, and an attorney may not be willing to take on a client with what could be an uphill battle.

The evidence gathered for tort law cases, even failed ones, can be used by lawmakers to pass new legislation protecting the public. This is what happened in 1965 when US senator Gaylord Nelson, who was backing a tire safety bill, brought out evidence he'd found from previous lawsuits about tires, which led to the Tire Safety Act of 1966.

Tort lawsuits about sensitive personal issues, such as racial discrimination or sexual abuse, give other people who have been wronged courage to come forward. The movie *Spotlight* (2015) was based on the true story of an investigation into widespread sexual abuse and coverups by the Catholic Church in Boston. At first, one woman informed an attorney named Mitchell Garabedian about her children being abused by a priest. This led to a domino effect of others coming forward. Garabedian wound up representing eighty-six of the priest's alleged rape and sexual abuse victims. The case resulted in a $10 million settlement in 2002 for the victims of the priest. In 2003, Garabedian represented 120 victims of 40 different priests and won an $85 million settlement from the Archdiocese of Boston.

The Power of the Ballot Box

There are other ways we can fight against corporate power, and it begins at the ballot box. One way Americans can try to take control of their country away from a political system run by corporations and special interests is to support third-party candidates (or major party candidates who are less beholden to special interests).

Ralph Nader's fight against the corporate domination of America extends beyond ordinary corporations. He was always very aware of the power corporate interests have over government. That was one thing about the two-party political system that increasingly bothered him as the years passed. Though Democrats and Republicans were different in many of the things they stood for, in his view they were both too closely controlled by corporate donations and corporate interests. Were they fighting for average Americans or for the large companies?

That question was one of the factors that motivated Nader to run for president in 1996, as a third-party candidate. Americans deserved another choice beyond the two major parties.

Nader is one of the most notable people to challenge the two-party system, but he was certainly not the first. People have longed for more electoral choices for a long time. There have been many presidential elections with more than two major candidates since the nineteenth century. In 1912, former Republican president Theodore Roosevelt ran for president again, this time as a "Bull Moose" Party (Progressive) candidate—and he actually did far better than the incumbent Republican, William Howard Taft. Roosevelt got eighty-eight electoral votes to Taft's eight, but they both lost to Democrat Woodrow Wilson. Also competing that year was Eugene V. Debs, who ran on the Socialist Party ticket and got nine hundred thousand votes.

In 1968, George Wallace ran as an American Independent and received almost ten million votes (13.5 percent of the popular vote) and forty-six electoral votes. In 1980, John Anderson ran as an Independent against Ronald Reagan and Jimmy Carter and received nearly six million votes, a total of 6.6 percent of the popular vote. In 1992, billionaire Ross Perot ran against George H. W. Bush and Bill Clinton and received nineteen million votes.

As Nader himself has pointed out, everyone who runs in an election thinks they are the best candidate and a spoiler to the other candidates. Everyone in any competition of any kind wants to win, and spoil the others' chances of winning. From spelling bees to cooking competitions, everyone else who is in the running is a potential spoiler to your chances of winning.

In 2016, Gary Johnson ran on the Libertarian Party ticket and received 4.4 million votes (a big improvement over the 1.3 million votes he got in the 2012 election). Jill Stein got nearly 1.5 million votes as the Green Party candidate, triple the votes she got in the 2012 election.

Third-party candidates can invigorate a stale two-party system and bring new ideas into the mainstream. Even if the candidates fail, their ideas can live on and gain in popularity over the years. Third parties in the nineteenth century were first against slavery, for women's right to vote, and for worker and farmer rights. They never won a national election, but their reforms were later adopted by one or both of the major political parties. Most importantly, third-party candidates remind us that there is always a choice, and we are bound by no rules as to who we vote for. If the Electoral College system is ever abolished, third-party candidates will have a real chance of winning elections, because people will not be as "afraid" to vote for them.

All Elections Matter

But it's not just presidential elections that make a difference, and it's not just third-party candidates who can matter. There are so many elected officials who can change the counties, cities, and states in which we live. Many people who vote do not exercise their full rights; they only vote for the "top" slots on the ballot and skip what they see as less important ones. But every vote counts for every position. Family court judges, town supervisors, county executives, local mayors, and council members—each elected official can make an impact, and it's up to us to research every one of them, and their positions and records. Each elected official has power and control over different aspects of our lives, and each one can play a role in helping us take back our government and our country from corporations.

The top 1 percent of the US population accounts for more than 20 percent of the county's income. That statistic is pretty frightening, because the wealthy control these huge corporations lobbying Congress to pass laws that favor their businesses. But all is not lost for the average citizen. One percent may control much of the country's wealth—but as Ralph Nader writes in his book *Breaking Through Power*, just 1 percent (or less) of the population can also force major changes to make our country and world safer and healthier. They can put more money into the pockets of the average person instead of the already wealthy. It does not take over 50 percent, or 40 percent, or even 10 percent. Just 1 percent.

How can this happen? How is it possible? Think of it this way: if you live in a town with a population of ten thousand, 1 percent of that number is one hundred. Imagine that a large chain store wants to open a branch on Main Street in your town of ten thousand. One hundred people show up to town meetings, each of them speaking out against the proposed store.

THIS TEXT IS FROM A SPEECH BY FORMER president and then third-party presidential candidate Theodore Roosevelt in 1912, where he explains how his opponent, Woodrow Wilson, stood for allowing corporate power to go unchecked, making the average person suffer at the hands of the wealthy and powerful. Third-party candidates have often stood against corporate power and the overall two-party political system in general.

The difference between Mr. Wilson [the Democratic presidential nominee] and myself is fundamental. The other day in a speech at Sioux Falls, Mr. Wilson stated his position when he said that the history of government, the history of liberty, was the history of the limitation of governmental power. This is true as an academic

Theodore Roosevelt campaigning for president on the 2012 Progressive party ticket.

*statement of history in the past. It is not true as
a statement affecting the present. It is true of the
history of medieval Europe. It is not true of the
history of twentieth-century America.*

*In the days when all governmental power
existed exclusively in the king or in the baronage
and when the people had no shred of that power
in their own hands, then it undoubtedly was
true that the history of liberty was the history
of the limitation of the governmental power of
the outsiders who possessed that power. But
today, the people have, actually or potentially,
the entire governmental power. It is theirs
to use and to exercise, if they choose to use
and to exercise it. It offers the only adequate
instrument with which they can work for the
betterment, for the uplifting of the masses of
our people.*

The liberty of which Mr. Wilson speaks
today means merely the liberty of some great
trust magnate to do that which he is not
entitled to do. It means merely the liberty
of some factory owner to work haggard
women over-hours for under-pay and himself
to pocket the profits. It means the liberty of
the factory owner to close his operatives into
some crazy deathtrap on a top floor, where if
fire starts, the slaughter is immense. It means
the liberty of the big factory owner—who is
conscienceless, and unscrupulous—to work
his men and women under conditions which
[inaudible] their lives like an [inaudible]. It
means the liberty of even less conscientious
factory owners to make their money out of the
toil, the labor, of little children. Men of this
stamp are the men whose liberty would be

preserved by Mr. Wilson. Men of this stamp are the men whose liberty would be preserved by the limitation of governmental power.

We propose, on the contrary, to extend governmental power in order to secure the liberty of the wage workers, of the men and women who toil in industry, to save the liberty of the oppressed from the oppressor. Mr. Wilson stands for the liberty of the oppressor to oppress. We stand for the limitation of his liberty not to oppress those who are weaker than himself.

A John Anderson pin from his 1980 presidential campaign and a Ross Perot pin from his 1992 campaign.

Picture an average classroom with twenty-five kids. Now multiply that by four. That's a lot of people voicing their opinions. If each of those hundred people spoke for just five minutes at a town meeting, that would be eight hours of protests, producing a definite impact! Imagine if those hundred people and wrote emails or called their town's mayor and board members. Imagine if those hundred people reflected public opinion in the town and protested in front of the site where the store was to go, or in front of the corporate headquarters. That level of support could be enough to make a difference and stop the store owners from opening up on Main Street.

Now imagine the population of your state—let's say you live in Colorado, population 5.7 million. One percent of that is fifty-seven thousand. Imagine there is some law in the state that needs to be changed, and imagine if the governor and members of the state legislature got fifty-seven thousand phone calls and emails and letters. If every one of those one percent made a ten second phone call to register their disapproval, one after another, they would keep the phones tied up for 158 hours straight!

And fifty-seven thousand emails would be enough to clog any email system. It would be overwhelming—and a powerful statement that would be hard to ignore.

And think of this—the population of the United States is 327 million, so 1 percent is 3.27 million people! Just 1 percent of the country's population mobilized against an unsafe corporation or unjust law would make all the difference. To realize how much of a difference 1 percent can make, you just have to look at elections—for example, in 2016, Trump beat Clinton by a third of 1 percent in Michigan, a little less than 1 percent in Wisconsin, and by just over 1 percent in Pennsylvania—for a total of forty-six electoral votes!

In 2016, only 61.4 percent of eligible voters actually voted in the United States. That sounds high, but it means that over one hundred million people who could have voted didn't. Donald Trump received sixty-three million votes and Hillary Clinton received sixty-six million votes. If all eligible voters had voted, they could have elected a third candidate as president just with their votes alone! Apathy is a big problem in America. There are twenty-five developed

A 1978 poster for a Ralph Nader–sponsored citizens' event about energy.

countries around the world where voter turnout is at a higher percentage than in the US.

Too many people in this country say, "I don't vote because my vote doesn't count," or "Nothing will ever change so why bother?," or "Who wins or loses does not affect me." Those kinds of arguments are dangerous. Every vote counts, and anything can change if enough people make it so. For example, doesn't having a living minimum wage affect lots of working families? If enough people vote for change, then things like a decent minimum wage will be enacted. And the important thing to realize is that candidates don't even have to win an election to make a difference. Sometimes a loss can motivate people to get more involved and push back. This is partly what happened during the 2018 election, where the Democrats took back the House of Representatives by winning forty-one Republican seats in the aftermath of the 2016 election.

Public Hearings

Your vote can fight corporate power in many ways. Control of the House and Senate determines what Congress does about potential product safety concerns. A congressional investigation into a corporation, or its products, can lead to people from that corporation being called before Congress to testify in a public hearing. The party that controls each body of Congress is the one that controls each of its committees, and therefore controls what hearings to hold. Such hearings can bring issues to light and put pressure on a corporation to do what's right, or even lead to new laws. In 2007, the CEO of toymaker Mattel was called before House and Senate consumer safety subcommittees to testify about hazardous toys and problems with their recalls. In 2019, two House subcommittees of the House Energy and Commerce Committee held a hearing on "Keeping Kids and Consumers Safe from Dangerous Products," which included seven different bills ranging from the Safer Occupancy Furniture Flammability Act that updated a standard to omit the need for potentially dangerous flame-retardant chemicals, to the Safe Cribs Act of 2019 that prohibited the manufacture and sale of crib bumpers.

Bill Murray and Ralph Nader during the Saturday Night Live 'Week-end Update' sketch, 1980.

CHAPTER TWELVE

PEOPLE PRESSURE = CHANGE FOR THE BETTER

BETWEEN LAWSUITS, VOTING, AND EVERYTHING else each of us can do to have an impact as an individual, things can change for the better. There are plenty of things you as one person can do to fight corporate power—but there are also plenty of things you can do as part of a larger group.

The strength of numbers can make for a powerful opponent to large corporate interests. There are hundreds of groups out there who support important causes and have power in their numbers of members. FlyersRights is an airline passenger consumer group that was formed in 2007 to protect passengers from being mistreated by airlines. Moms

Demand Action is a gun violence prevention organization that is an offshoot of Everytown for Gun Safety, another citizen organization. Other groups that promote important causes include: Mothers Against Drunk Driving (MADD), Students Against Destructive Decisions (SADD), Common Cause, and Student Public Interest Research Groups (PIRGs, proposed and assisted by Ralph Nader). A group called the Nuclear Freeze Coalition helped pressure the Reagan government to adopt an arms reduction treaty. Some groups even represent an entire slice of the public, such as the American Association of Retired Persons (AARP) whose membership is open to anyone over the age of fifty. They have thirty-eight million members!

The powerful tobacco industry has faced restrictions based on pressure from groups like the American Cancer Society, the American Lung Association, the Campaign for Tobacco-Free Kids, and from the government. Over the last fifty years, there have been major consumer victories against tobacco companies in the United States. Warning labels explaining the risks of disease from smoking had to be put on cigarette packs. Tobacco companies were no longer allowed to advertise on television.

But these victories were not enough. Telling people that they could become sick from smoking and limiting advertising did not solve a major problem—the fact that smoking is an activity that causes direct harm to others, too. Because cigarette smoke (which contains over seven thousand chemicals) is emitted and exhaled from lit cigarettes and cigars, it can be breathed in by anyone nearby. The Centers for Disease Control and Prevention (CDC) estimates that since 1964, 2.5 million nonsmokers have died. "There is no risk-free level of secondhand smoke exposure," they state. "Even brief exposure can be harmful to health."

Over the years, smoking has been banned from most public buildings, most workplaces, from airlines, trains and buses, most restaurants, bars, hotel rooms, and even from public outdoor spaces like plazas. Think about where you see people smoking these days— almost no place except the street and in their own homes. This is not because 50 percent of the population put pressure on their lawmakers or on the tobacco companies. It was a small

FROM THE CENTERS FOR DISEASE CONTROL (CDC) WEBSITE:

SMOKING LEADS TO DISEASE AND DISABILITY and harms nearly every organ of the body.

- More than sixteen million Americans are living with a disease caused by smoking.
- For every person who dies because of smoking, at least thirty people live with a serious smoking-related illness.
- Smoking causes cancer, heart disease, stroke, lung diseases, diabetes, and chronic obstructive pulmonary disease (COPD), which includes emphysema and chronic bronchitis.
- Smoking also increases risk for tuberculosis, certain eye diseases, and problems of the immune system, including rheumatoid arthritis.

Smoking is the leading cause
of preventable death.

- Worldwide, tobacco use causes more than
  seven million deaths per year. If the pattern
  of smoking all over the globe doesn't
  change, more than eight million people a
  year will die from diseases related to tobacco
  use by 2030.
- Cigarette smoking is responsible for more
  than 480,000 deaths per year in the United
  States, including more than 41,000 deaths
  resulting from secondhand smoke exposure.
  This is about one in five deaths annually, or
  1,300 deaths every day.
- On average, smokers die ten years earlier
  than nonsmokers.

- If smoking continues at the current rate among US youth, 5.6 million of today's Americans younger than eighteen years of age are expected to die prematurely from a smoking-related illness. This represents about one in every thirteen Americans aged seventeen years or younger who are alive today.

Smoking costs the United States billions of dollars each year.

- Total economic cost of smoking is more than $300 billion a year, including nearly $170 billion in direct medical care for adults, and more than $156 billion in lost productivity due to premature death and exposure to secondhand smoke.

The tobacco industry spends billions of dollars each year on cigarette and smokeless tobacco advertising and promotions.

- $9.06 billion was spent on advertising and promotion of cigarettes and smokeless tobacco combined—about $25 million every day, and more than $1 million every hour.

- Price discounts to retailers account for 73.3 percent of all cigarette marketing (about $6.16 billion). These are discounts paid in order to reduce the price of cigarettes to consumers.

State spending on tobacco prevention and control does not meet CDC-recommended levels.

- States have billions of dollars from the taxes they put on tobacco products and money from lawsuits against cigarette companies that they can use to prevent smoking and help smokers quit. Right now, though, the states only use a very small amount of that money to prevent and control tobacco use.
- In fiscal year 2020, states will collect $27.2 billion from tobacco taxes and settlements in court, but will only spend $740 million in the same year. That's only 2.7 percent spent on programs that can stop young people from becoming smokers and help current smokers quit.
- Right now, not a single state out of fifty funds these programs at CDC's "recommended" level. Only three states (Alaska, California, and Maine) give even 70

percent of the full recommended amount. Twenty-eight states and the District of Columbia spend less than 20 percent of what the CDC recommends. One state, Connecticut, gives no state funds for prevention and quit-smoking programs.

- Spending 12 percent (about $3.3 billion) of the $27.2 billion would fund every state's tobacco control program at CDC-recommended levels.

For years, the tobacco industry advertised that their products were harmless and were smoked by doctors.

fraction of people who made the difference, backed by growing public opinion. They pushed and pushed until the tide turned, and smoking was recognized as a real nuisance. Thanks to these changes, and a dramatic decline overall in smoking (from 45 percent of the population in 1965 to 15 percent in 2020), the number of nonsmokers with measurable nicotine biproducts in their system from secondhand smoke exposure went from 90 percent down to 25 percent between 1988 and 2011. This is not the result of the tobacco industry willingly doing anything, nor of state legislatures and Congress acting on their own—it's the result of average people who seriously act to make a difference.

As corporations get more powerful and have tighter control over members of Congress, it becomes more difficult to have an effect. The gun industry is one area where it's been difficult to make any progress. Hundreds of school shootings and promises of tighter restrictions on guns later, little has happened. People power is needed to fight against corporate lobbyists from groups like the National Rifle Association, who influenced more than forty states to prevent municipalities from passing certain types of gun safety laws. So it is true, groups can be powerful—on both sides of an issue. And sometimes it is the group with more members and political connections that can "speak" the loudest.

Unions and Guilds

People power is about individuals who want to make a change, because all change starts with one person and builds from there into a snowball effect. One person becomes a few becomes many. And many people can win elections and make change happen. As we've seen already, individuals can certainly take on corporations using the power of their vote. But many people united together for a common cause can make an even greater impact in being heard. Just at a time when corporations were first becoming large and powerful, workers banded together to form unions. They realized that if only one or two or ten workers out of hundreds or thousands complained about working conditions or wages, nothing would be done. But what if almost everyone in a certain field belonged to a workers' organization? That would be powerful!

Many unions are groups of people in the same profession—auto workers, teachers, police, garment workers. Other unions consist of different groups of workers. Unions have accomplished a great deal for workers over the years, including pay raises, shorter work weeks, the end of child labor, unemployment benefits, safer workplaces, and workers compensation laws.

The oldest union in the country is the Brotherhood of Locomotive Engineers and Trainmen, founded in 1863. The American Federation of Labor (AFL) was founded in 1884 by Samuel Gompers. It grew into a huge organization called the AFL-CIO, made up of fifty-five unions around the country and the world, with a membership of twelve million people. Some of the large unions that are part of the AFL-CIO are the International Brotherhood of Electrical Workers, United Steelworkers of America, American Federation of Government Employees, National Association of Letter Carriers, and the United Food and Commercial Workers International Union. Workers' groups cover pretty much every type of occupation, including authors and actors—the Screen Actors Guild has 160,000 members.

Luckily for workers of all types, unions in the 1930s and 1940s became nearly as large and powerful as the corporations and industries they were intended to protect workers from. They helped protect the average citizen from being taken advantage of by both corporations and the government. In the years since, unions have declined in power and membership due to automation, the exporting of jobs overseas, and anti-union laws.

Protest Power

Throughout history, one of the most powerful ways people have made their voices heard is by gathering together and taking action for their cause. The famous Boston Tea Party of 1773 was an early example of an American protest; colonists angry over taxation dumped hundreds of crates of imported tea into Boston Harbor. In 1913, a Women's Suffragette Parade of eight thousand people marched in Washington, DC, to demand that women have the right to vote. After that, the nation's capital became a regular site of protest. The March on Washington in

1963 saw 250,000 people come together to rally for civil rights. In January 2017, the day after Donald Trump's inauguration, millions of people participated in the Women's March in DC and numerous other cities around the country.

More recently in 2020, for weeks after the brutal death of a Black man named George Floyd in Minneapolis, Minnesota, under the knee of a police officer (both a crime and a tort), thousands of Americans in hundreds of cities coast to coast held protests to demand an end to police brutality and racism, and to insist that Black Lives Matter. These protests grew and spread into a sub-movement to remove statues of Confederate generals (who were fighting to preserve slavery) from cities around the nation, as well as other racist-themed monuments.

Protests such as these sometimes are just the beginning of a movement, and sometimes directly cause change to occur. Ultimately, Americans can inspire change through the ballot box, but waiting that long is often not an option, especially when something dramatic propels public anger. Protests can make change happen in the moment by putting immense pressure on federal, state, or local governments to do something. In 2020, this included changing law enforcement procedures and creating more safeguards to protect citizens from police violence. Some also suggested defunding the police budget and using that money for other agencies and departments that can provide social services to help citizens. In July 2020, the New York City Council passed a measure that would reduce the New York City Police Department's funding by $1 billion and redistribute that money to other city agencies.

Boycott Power

There is another way we the people can control and contain corporations—by boycotting their products if we feel they promote unfair practices. One notable business that has been boycotted by some people in recent years is the fast food eatery Chick-fil-A, because of their donations of millions of dollars to anti-gay groups. In July 2020, hundreds of companies began a month-long boycott of Facebook, removing their ads from the social media site in protest of how they felt Facebook mishandled hate speech. Boycotts can put pressure on companies to reconsider their positions—but usually the financial dent of a boycott is not as bad as the public relations dent that happens when news media covers the stories. Companies don't want to look bad.

More Oversight, Not Less

As mentioned in chapter 1, Ralph Nader was the driving force behind many consumer protection laws, regulations, and agencies. Oversight is another way that "group" power can regulate corporations, these are just different kinds of groups. Official commissions and task forces are much-needed strong arms of the federal government that focus on specific issues. The Consumer Product Safety Commission (CPSC), for example, administers and enforces federal laws related to product safety. According to its website: "These laws authorize the agency to protect the public against unreasonable risks of injuries and deaths associated with consumer products." Some of the laws enforced by the agency are the Consumer Product Safety Act, the Children's Gasoline Burn Prevention Act, Federal Hazardous Substances Act, Child Safety Protection Act, Flammable Fabrics Act, Poison Prevention Packaging Act, and Child Nicotine Poisoning Prevention Act of 2015. In

2009, the CPSC fined toymaker Mattel $2.3 million for violating a 1978 federal ban on toys with more than .06 percent lead by weight in paint. The ability to fine companies helps ensure compliance with safety regulations, but it does not mean people injured by their unsafe products can't sue. They can!

Overall, there's a whole array of people-power tactics that can be a good check on the power of corporations and the government representatives who would prefer to shield them.

Ralph Nader explains a famous case of consumer protection in which a woman was severely burned by a cup of coffee at MacDonald's.

CHAPTER THIRTEEN

THE TORT LAW MUSEUM AND THE FUTURE OF CIVIL ACTION

The Tort Law Museum

People power is a critical part of our country's future. If we are to thrive as a democracy, we have to not only participate in people power, but we also have to celebrate and encourage it. The best way to do that is to spread the word by teaching Americans about tools of justice, such as tort law.

In northwestern Connecticut, just a few miles south of the Massachusetts border, a very unique museum opened in 2015—the American Museum of Tort Law. Opening a museum dedicated to tort law was a longtime dream for Ralph Nader, who has spent his life fighting against corporate power to ensure that the common person was represented and heard. Nader was visiting an attorney in Boulder, Colorado, one day in the 1990s, when he asked what happens to the various graphic exhibits that are put on display during a trial. The attorney said they were tossed into the trash after the trial. It seemed like a terrible waste, and this gave Nader the idea of creating a place where mementos of important cases could live forever and teach people of all ages about the importance of civil lawsuits.

He looked into it further and was shocked to discover that there was no law museum in existence anywhere. Of the thirty-five thousand museums in the United States, there was almost everything else under the sun! There were museums dedicated to clocks, mustard, hammers, barbershops, potatoes, bananas, salt and pepper shakers, Pez candy dispensers, yoyos, carousels, funerals, beer cans, and hair, but there was no law museum. The time was ripe, but for years, Nader's dream remained only on paper. Creating a museum is not so simple because it takes money, space, and a team of talented people. In the years that followed, Nader continued to rally support for his law museum. In a concept paper for the proposed museum, professor Joseph A. Page of the Georgetown University Law Center wrote in 2013, "An American Museum of Tort Law should convey to the general public its stake in the civil justice system."

Nader found an ideal location in his hometown: the old Winsted Savings Bank building on Main Street, a place that had been around for many decades. Nader and his friends and supporters raised $3 million to fix up the bank and transform it into a museum. After the transformation was complete, the American Museum of Tort Law opened in Winsted in September 2015. Among the notables in the crowd of nine hundred people was Nader's friend, the singer Patti Smith, who campaigned for president with Nader in 2000. She sang two songs for the audience.

The American Tort Law Museum is the first law museum of any kind in the country, celebrating the constitutional right to a civil trial by jury. Almost every other museum in existence deals with a collection of physical things. Physical things are easy to display, whether artworks or rocks or coins or bananas. But the law is a concept. Making eye-catching and interesting exhibits on tort law was a challenge. However, displaying some of the things that were the subjects of famous lawsuits was possible. Featured in the museum is a restored red 1963 Chevrolet Corvair, one of the cars at the center of Ralph Nader's movement against unsafe vehicles in the 1960s. It may have been cheaper and easier to find an old rusty version of the car to put on display, but the point was to show visitors just how attractive the car looked to the average person when it was shiny and new—to illustrate how beneath its beauty hid deadly dangers. There is also a room featuring dangerous vintage toys that were the subject of lawsuits.

Still, it was not possible to fill the museum only with things that were the subject of lawsuits. Those would be nice visuals, but there had to be displays that illustrated key ideas behind the important cases. Nader thought back to the courtroom case exhibits he saw in Colorado years before and how they were designed to convey important ideas to the jury. He realized he had to do the same thing for the museum—make visitors understand the cases with pictures, not just words. He enlisted graphic artists, led by Pulitzer Prize–winning

The American Museum of Tort Law in Winsted, Connecticut, is housed inside a former bank.

artist Matt Wuerker, to bring historic cases to life and create fun, interesting, and colorful graphics showing the main ideas. In a way, the museum is like an art museum—with legal cases and concepts converted into artworks that are easy to understand and interesting to look at, and with probing questions to stimulate further thinking.

For the important position of museum director, Nader hired a former tort attorney named Richard Newman, who was at the time volunteering for environmental groups and saw a post about the new museum. Intrigued, Newman wrote to Nader offering his services, and six months later, he found himself heading up the museum. Newman works closely with Nader to arrange special events and help the museum grow. The museum's brochure proclaims: "We hope that the Museum will inspire a sense of future possibilities for the well-being of both our fellow citizens and for our society. Isn't it good to see how Tort Law enables the little guys to bring the big boys to justice for causing wrongful injuries?"

One of the museum's galleries features displays about precedent-setting cases in the history of tort law. Another gallery focuses on dangerous toys, including a once-popular Fisher-Price school bus set (choking hazard) and darts (sharp!). The main gallery has displays on high-profile cases, including a detailed display on the story of Ralph Nader and his (and others') fight against the automobile makers to push for improved car safety.

The museum highlights some recent cases that may have been misinterpreted by the public from their negative (or simply inadequate) coverage in the media. One such case is the famous "hot coffee case," a.k.a. *Liebeck v. McDonald's Restaurants* (see chapter 4). The museum display tells the whole story and reveals all the facts of the case, showing in words and pictures that this was not some careless old lady trying to game the system and get rich from an accidental spill.

Nader's personal favorites include the tobacco and asbestos exhibits because of the large class of victims those cases cover (millions of people), as well as the dangerous toys exhibit because it introduces kids to tort principles of negligence and wrongful injury. Indeed, the author remembers playing with the same exact Fisher-Price school bus that is on display in the museum!

A vintage Chevrolet Corvair inside the museum.

(*Right*) Part of the museum display on the famous "hot coffee case."

Special events at the museum bring specific tort law cases and topics into focus. In April 2016, the museum held a program with special guest speakers Mitchell Garabedian, the attorney in the infamous Boston priest scandal (he was portrayed by Stanley Tucci in the Oscar-winning 2015 movie, *Spotlight*, based on the true story of his case); and Jan Schlichtmann, who was the subject of *A Civil Action*, a book about an environmental tort law case that later became a movie (in which Schlichtmann was portrayed by John Travolta).

The first "Tort Law Education Day" was held at the American Museum of Tort Law on October 5, 2019. It was a day to celebrate and demonstrate the power of the people against big corporations. There was a keynote address by US senator Sheldon Whitehouse of Rhode Island, who explained how big and powerful corporations were trying to get control of the Supreme Court by backing certain nominees with lots of money and pressuring Congress to vote to confirm their preferred choices. There were also numerous speakers on every variety of tort—from sports to medicine to the environment. One of the speakers was a young woman named Kristen Rose, who in 2012 was badly injured in a terrible car accident

Ralph Nader speaks at the Museum's Tort Law Education Day 2019.

due to a faulty tire that had been recalled more than ten years earlier (she needed ninety-seven staples and fourteen stitches). She later sued the tire company and the car manufacturer, among others, and received money through settlements with several of the defendants. As a result of her accident and recovery, and the learning process of filing a lawsuit and fighting for her rights, she started a non-profit organization called Auto Accident Survivors of Georgia to help raise awareness about tire safety and tire recalls. Her case showed how even when it's not clear who is to blame, there still has to be accountability. She was owed compensation for her pain whether from one company or from several others who shared the blame.

One of the museum's goals is to give a voice to people like Kristen, who have been harmed and, in a search for compensation for their injuries, find themselves up against huge companies such as Bridgestone and Ford, companies that have money, power, and resources to fight lawsuits. The common theme throughout the museum is celebrating the power of the average person thanks to the right to a trial by jury. Ralph Nader and the museum's founders and supporters hope that by celebrating the rights of common people, the museum can inspire more people out there who have been wrongfully injured but feel powerless to take action.

School groups often visit the museum; one special visit was made in 2019 by twenty-eight law and American Studies students from the Gilbert School, a local high school from which Ralph Nader graduated in 1951. The museum has been visited by numerous other students from all across the area, including college students from Northeastern University, Mount Holyoke College, and Trinity College; law school students from the University of Massachusetts, the University of Connecticut, Harvard, and Yale; and paralegal students from the University of Hartford.

"The museum sounds wonderful and will be of vital importance to our citizenry should they take the time to appreciate its benefits," said former Supreme Court justice Sandra Day O'Connor. She had a point—when the museum opened, there were many positive reviews and news stories about it, but it's very important that Americans continue to appreciate the museum and its mission. In 2017, Supreme Court justice

Stephen Breyer toured the museum and called it "an excellent educational institution."

An Increased Online Presence for Changing Times

Since its opening, the museum's website has always been a place to learn more about tort law. With the pandemic in 2020, the museum, like hundreds of others around the country, had to close indefinitely. But the museum's important mission still had to be carried out, and so the museum director worked with his team to create a virtual tour of the museum, taking many of the important cases from a physical display to a web-based version. Exhibits on famous cases, dangerous toys, precedent-setting cases, and the story of Ralph Nader's fight against General Motors are all online with the same colorful graphics that are on display inside the physical museum. The museum also maintains an active presence on social media, where frequent posts keep followers informed of the latest news in tort law case rulings and related topics. During the pandemic, the museum also held virtual tort law events to temporarily replace in-person lectures.

Destroying the Myth of Frivolous Lawsuits

One of the goals of the Tort Law museum, and of those people who support it, is to dispel the myth of fraudulent and frivolous lawsuits. The tort law system has been threatened by this myth, and reforms would limit people's rights to sue.

Pretty much any item can be dangerous if used the wrong way. A doll that passes safety checks is not meant to be used to smack someone in the face. There is a line between legitimate and frivolous lawsuits. Most people apply common sense when filing lawsuits, and most attorneys are smart enough to know a real case versus an exaggerated or false claim. If a frivolous lawsuit is filed, chances are it won't make it very far. In his book, *Floored!*, slip and fall expert witness Russell Kendzior estimates that just 3 percent of slip and fall cases are fraudulent.

It's true that anyone can file a lawsuit against anyone else about pretty much anything. But that doesn't mean the lawsuit will succeed. Civil Rule 11 of the United States Federal Rules of Civil Procedure says that, in filing a lawsuit, an attorney has to certify that the suit is not being presented "for any improper purpose, such as to harass, cause unnecessary delay, or needlessly increase the cost of litigation," that the claims are warranted by existing law or a nonfrivolous argument for changing an existing law, and that the factual contentions have evidence supporting them. Violating this rule could result in punishment of the attorney. Judges control their courtrooms and can affirm a motion to dismiss a case.

In this day and age where money is so important, people get jealous and angry when they hear about large jury awards for things they view as frivolous. But if it was that easy, we could all make millions every time we spilled something on ourselves. Tort law cases revolve around key details. If I were to fall on a supermarket floor, I'd have no case if the floor was dry and clean. Maybe I just lost my balance because I was dizzy. There would be no way for me to blame the store. Similarly, if there was a drop or two of water on the floor, that would not be enough for me to blame my fall on. However, a visibly wet and slippery floor with no warning sign is another story. And what if the wet and slippery floor had a sign, but the sign was a few feet too far away? Or facing the wrong direction? Or in English only and I am a Spanish speaker?

All of these are potentially complicating factors that would require a jury to think carefully. The circumstance of where the fall happens can also be a factor. You wouldn't expect wet conditions on a supermarket floor, but if you fell in a shallow splash pool at a water park, would you have a case against the water park? Let's rewind for a moment though—if I lost my balance in the supermarket because I was momentarily dizzy on account of a wrongly prescribed medication, I might have a case—not against the store but against my doctor.

If you are in City Hall and there is a large bulge in the floor causing you to trip and fall, that could be a case. You'd have a reasonable expectation that the floor would be level. But if you were in a city-owned park and you tripped on a little mound of grass, that's not the same at all because it's a park and you expect the ground to be uneven.

The other factor is just how injured you are. If you fall and hurt your ankle but the pain goes away the next day and you can still do all your normal activities, it would be hard to prove some kind of monetary damage is owed to you. If you fall and cannot walk or use your right arm for four weeks, that could be a major inconvenience.

Jurors are not stupid. Most of the time, they award money to a plaintiff when a real "wrong" was done. Jurors are average people like you, and what goes through their heads during a successful plaintiff argument is often "That could have been me, and I need to send a message to the defendant so this does not happen again." Destroying the myth of frivolous lawsuits is key to making sure that tort deform does not take hold and wreck people's ability to file civil lawsuits.

It's Right to Fight Corporate Power

So what does the future hold for tort law and people power?

The American Museum of Tort Law arrived at a critical time in our history. It is meant not only as a museum showing things that happened in the past, but also as living celebration of tort law, a reminder that the law works for the present and future, with old perils and new ones alike.

Ralph Nader hopes that "learning about tort law and its memorable cases becomes part of high school education for everyone—which would include fine print contracts that take away right to trial by jury and going to court

(compulsory arbitration clause, for example)."
He adds, "Citizen groups need to be formed in
every state to rescue tort law from tort deform
and expand its reach for new values (privacy),
new technologies (biotech, nanotech, artificial
intelligence) and increase its pathetically low
utilization (one or two percent)."

It's true—according to a Rand Institute for
Civil Justice study, only 10 percent of wrongfully
injured people file a claim or complaint, and only
2 percent of injured people actually file a lawsuit.

Nader has said, "Hear this practicing plaintiff
lawyers, wherever you are: you number sixty
thousand strong in the US. If you each speak
to small groups (classes, clubs, reunions, etc.)
totaling some thousand people a year, that
is sixty million people receiving knowledge
central to their quality of life and security. Every
year! Fascinating human interest stories full of
courage, persistence, and vindication of critical
rights will captivate and inspire your audiences."

Sadly, politicians who suggest that
corporations have too much power and want to
enforce more regulations are called names by
their opponents. In the fall of 2019, news stories
circulated that Democratic donors from Wall

Street were so scared of candidate Elizabeth Warren's proposed corporate policies that they would actually consider donating to Trump instead if she were the nominee. Stories like this prove how frightened corporate America is of change, of anything that would cut into their profits. It's important to remember that many of President Franklin D. Roosevelt's New Deal policies created new ways to oversee a financial system that had gone out of control without a safety net.

There is nothing wrong with keeping corporations in check and making them answer to the same standards and rules that the average citizen has to answer to. The government answers to us, is elected by us, and serves at our pleasure. Like our government, corporations exist to serve us. The people. We have to remember that corporations need us. They provide us with products and services we pay for. Without us as their customers, they would not exist. Corporate America will listen, if we speak up. People power is about exploring all the ways we can make our voices heard and create powerful and lasting change.

Selected Bibliography

Bogus, Carl T. *Why Lawsuits are Good for America*. New York: New York University Press, 2001.

Bowman, Joan. "American Museum of Tort Law Curriculum Guide," American Museum of Tort Law. https://www.tortmuseum.org/wp-content/uploads/2020/04/Curriculum-Guide-Package_Complete.pdf.

Coughlin, Dennis J. *Crashing the 737 MAX, Volume I*. Independently published, 2019.

Mintz, Morton and Jerry S. Cohen. *Power, Inc*. New York: Bantam Books, 1977.

Hallam, Henry. *The Constitutional History of England from the Accession of Henry VII to the Death of George II*. Cambridge, UK: Cambridge University Press.

Koenig, Thomas H. and Michael L. Rustad. *In Defense of Tort Law*. New York: New York University Press, 2001.

Drivon, Lawrence E. *The Civil War on Consumer Rights*. Berkeley: Conari Press, 1990.

Cambre, Megan E. "A Single Symbolic Dollar: How Nominal Damages Can Keep Lawsuits Alive," *Georgia Law Review* 52, no. 3 (2018).

Kendzior, Russell J. *Floored! Real-Life Stories from a Slip and Fall Expert Witness*. Lanham, MD: Rowman & Littlefield, 2017.

Nader, Ralph. *Unsafe at Any Speed*. New York: Bantam Books, 1973.

Nader, Ralph. *The Seventeen Traditions*. New York: HarperCollins Publishers, 2007.

Nader, Ralph *Breaking Through Power*. San Francisco: City Lights Books, 2016.

Nader, Ralph. *The Good Fight*. New York: Regan Books, 2004.

Nader, Ralph. "Suing for Justice," *Harper's Magazine*, April 2016, 57–62.

Page, Joseph A. "Concept Paper for the American Museum of Tort Law." Washington: American Museum of Tort Law, 2013.

Zausner, Robert. *Bad Brake Ford Trucks Deadly When Parked*. Philadelphia: Camino Books, 2012.

Zausner, Robert. *Two Boys: Divided by Fortune—United by Tragedy*. Philadelphia: Camino Books, 2009.

Image Credits

Index